WILLIAMS-SONOMA

cooking for friends

AUTHORS

alison attenborough & jamie kimm

PHOTOGRAPHER

petrina tinslay

Oxmoor House®

contents

In our line of work, we have so many ideas about food running through our brains that we can't make use of all of them. Since we're both chefs and food stylists, and we both love what we do, we actually never take a break from thinking and talking about food. You might even call us obsessed. Every meal we eat at home or in a restaurant, every food magazine we flip through, every trip we take to the greengrocer's or the butcher's or upstate or abroad is another opportunity to find a clever trick of the trade. It might be a new way to present a favorite dish or an interesting flavor variation or even an unusual ingredient to try—just the kernel of an idea that we keep riffing on. We're constantly on the lookout for inspiration.

What do we like to cook at home for our friends? And most important, what keeps our friends coming back for more? Well, there are the dishes that we've been perfecting for years at dinner parties, whether a client's or our own, that unfailingly impress without elaborate or costly preparation, like fish cooked in parchment or grilled steak. Then, there are foods that we simply love and want to share with others, like Jamie's pestos and vinaigrettes and Alison's poached chicken soup and flavored creams. We like finding little ways to make cooking for friends a special experience.

The key to a fun, casual dinner party is to make food you love, to do as much as you can ahead of time, and to add some flair to the presentation. If you start with fresh, seasonal ingredients, you can't go wrong. Often, we're spontaneous and will decide one afternoon to invite friends over that same evening for homemade pizza. Everyone helps roll out the dough and add different toppings (arugula and prosciutto is our favorite), then we serve the pizzas on cutting boards and the wine in tumblers at the kitchen counter.

You may come across a few ingredients in these pages you've never heard of, and we encourage you to seek them out. We've found that a little extra effort pays big returns in the end, and it's worth it to elevate our dinner parties into something special for everyone. After all, your dinner party and the enjoyment of your friends is at stake.

Alison & Jamie

our approach to cooking for friends

We like to take a favorite ingredient or dish and make it special. "Four Ways" are recipes that we think are so fabulous, in one way or another, that we couldn't confine ourselves to giving you only one version. Some of the "Four Ways" collections are the dishes we've found over the years to be never-fail crowd-pleasers—and we've worked for some pretty demanding crowds in our time. Others are recipes we make all the time and that we often fall back on when company calls. If you want to throw a party but don't have much time, it's smart to start with a framework you're familiar with and then vary the flavors and style to suit the occasion. When cooking for friends, we usually strive to keep things simple, but never boring.

We always pay careful attention to the seasons, too. Not only do your dishes taste better when the ingredients have bloomed to ripeness in their natural season—and when they haven't traveled halfway around the globe to plop down, exhausted, on your dinner table—but they also help to make every party a celebration of the moment, of *these* people gathering at *this* time to enjoy one another's company. Keeping in touch with the seasons brings a delightful sense of rightness and comfort to whatever you serve. When guests come in with the tips of their noses bright red and stamping the snow from their boots, they don't want a martini and a light pasta. They want a hot toddy and some shepherd's pie to fortify them for the eventual journey home. To help you put together a meal for any time of the year, we've come up with eight different menus for each season, a mix of casual dinners, elegant suppers, and cocktail parties (pages 240 and 246). We love to mix and match dishes and encourage you to do the same. Try serving a variation of a side dish with cocktails, or a salad as a main course. You can also double a recipe here or there to accommodate a larger group.

Because we are also food stylists, whenever we share our food with friends, we like to make it look a little glamorous. To achieve that, we might use unusual arrangements or garnishes and serve our dishes in unique plates, bowls, or glassware. It gives our guests a lovely idea of what they can do at home. Some recipes in the book lent themselves to so many presentation possibilities that we were unable to settle on just one. Instead, we give you three or four ideas, and we show them to you in photographs, knowing that a picture often tells the story better than words.

All of these variations and choices and options are our way of saying, please feel free to play with your food. Play with the ingredients, the flavorings, and the way you arrange the food on the plate. And be sure to invite your friends over to play with you, because a jolly crowd of folks you like always makes mealtime more fun.

drinks

The key to a fun, casual party is how it starts. Even
if you've got some last-minute cooking to do, give guests
an effusive greeting and a nice cocktail the moment
they arrive and everyone will be happy.

We first tasted this version of a caipirinha, made with fresh passion fruit, on a trip to Brazil, the birthplace of both passion fruit and caipirinhas. And we couldn't get enough of it.

passion fruit caipirinha

. . . .

CHOOSING THE BOOZE

If you have a hard time finding *cachaça*, a Brazilian spirit made from sugarcane, you can substitute vodka to make the equally delicious caipiroska!

On your work surface, firmly press and roll lime with palm of your hand to release essential oils in rind and juices. Cut lime into 8 slices, then cut each slice in half. Place the pieces in an old-fashioned glass. Sprinkle with sugar and crush with a muddler. Scoop flesh from passion fruit halves into glass, add *cachaça,* and stir to mix. Add ice and serve at once.

lime 1

superfine sugar 2 tsp

passion fruit 1, halved

cachaça ¼ cup (2 fl oz)

ice

serves 1

ginger and ginger

. . . .

SERVE IT WITH

We like to serve this pungent concoction before an Asian menu. If you can't find ginger wine (it's very British), use all ginger beer. If you do locate the wine, make sure you try a splash of it in your lemonade (or whiskey) sometime.

Squeeze lime half into a cocktail shaker. Add fresh ginger and muddle together. Add ginger wine and ice, cover, and shake until well combined. Strain into an old-fashioned glass and top with ginger beer. Garnish with candied ginger and lemongrass stalk (if using) and serve at once.

lime ½

fresh ginger ½-inch piece

ginger wine 6 Tbsp (3 fl oz)

ice

ginger beer 6 Tbsp (3 fl oz)

candied ginger for garnish

lemongrass 1 stalk, trimmed, for garnish (optional)

serves 1

On a trip to Portugal, we had the good fortune of traveling to the vineyards of Taylor Fladgate. This was the winery's signature cocktail, called the "Chip and tonic," after their classic white port, Chip Dry. It's very light and refreshing, particularly in summer.

white port and tonic

· ·

ice

white port ¼ cup (2 fl oz)

tonic water 6 Tbsp (3 fl oz)

lemon or lime wedge
for garnish

serves 1

Fill an old-fashioned glass with ice. Add white port, top with tonic, and stir to mix. Garnish with citrus wedge and serve at once. Serve with a swizzle stick, if desired.

SERVE IT WITH

Try this with a little spread of Iberian appetizers, like *boquerones* (marinated white anchovies), Marcona almonds, and grilled *cipolline* (small, flat onions) and fennel.

lillet lemon

· ·

fresh mint 1 sprig

fresh lemon juice 1 Tbsp

ice

Lillet Blanc 3 Tbsp (1½ fl oz)

gin 3 Tbsp (1½ fl oz)

club soda (soda water)
splash

lemon twist for garnish

serves 1

In a cocktail shaker, gently muddle mint and lemon juice. Fill shaker half full with ice and add Lillet and gin. Cover and shake until well combined. Strain into a tumbler or old-fashioned glass filled with ice and top with a splash of club soda. Garnish with lemon twist and serve at once.

MAKE A SPLASH

To give your aperitif service a stylish air, let your guests add their own splash of club soda from little glass bottles, as if they were making *citron pressé* in a Parisian café, or from a charming vintage seltzer bottle.

watermelon and lime

. . . .

seedless watermelon
8 cups chunks, plus
6–8 wedges for garnish

fresh lime juice 1 cup,
plus thin lime slices for
garnish

sugar ½ cup

gold tequila 2 cups

Grand Marnier ½ cup
(4 fl oz)

ice

serves 6–8

In a blender, in batches, combine 4 cups water, watermelon, lime juice, and sugar. Blend on high until completely liquid and frothy. Transfer to a pitcher, add tequila and Grand Marnier, and stir to combine. Serve in individual glasses over ice. Garnish each glass with lime slices and a watermelon wedge.

cucumber and chile

. . . .

cucumbers 10, peeled,
seeded, and chopped,
plus 6–8 wedges for
garnish

fresh lime juice 1 cup

agave nectar or honey
2 Tbsp (1 fl oz)

serrano chile ½,
seeded and minced,
plus 6–8 whole chiles
for garnish (optional)

sea salt

silver tequila 2 cups

ice

serves 6–8

In a blender, in batches, combine 4½ cups water, cucumbers, lime juice, agave nectar, minced chile, and a generous pinch of salt. Blend on high until smooth. Strain through a fine-mesh sieve into a pitcher. Add tequila, stir well, and chill for at least 1 hour before serving. Serve in individual glasses over ice. Garnish each glass with a cucumber wedge and a chile (if using).

papaya and lime

....

papaya 5 cups chopped, plus cubes for garnish

fresh lime juice ⅓ cup (3 fl oz), plus 6–8 lime wedges for garnish

sugar 1 cup

gold tequila 2 cups

Grand Marnier ¼ cup (2 fl oz)

ice

serves 6–8

In a blender, in batches, combine 8 cups water, papaya, lime juice, and sugar. Blend on high until completely liquid and frothy. Transfer to a pitcher, add tequila and Grand Marnier, and stir to combine. Serve in individual glasses over ice. Garnish each glass with a lime wedge and a cocktail skewer of papaya cubes.

minted hibiscus and raspberry

....

raspberries 3 cups

fresh mint ¼ cup coarsely chopped, plus leaves for garnish

hibiscus tea 6 tea bags or 6 Tbsp hibiscus flowers

sugar ¾ cup

silver tequila 2 cups

Grand Marnier ½ cup (4 fl oz)

fresh lime juice ½ cup (4 fl oz)

ice

serves 6–8

In a large saucepan, bring 8 cups water to a boil. Add 2 cups raspberries, chopped mint, and tea bags. Remove from heat and let stand at room temperature for 1 hour. Remove tea bags and strain mixture through a fine-mesh sieve into a large pitcher. Discard solids. Add sugar, tequila, Grand Marnier, and lime juice and stir to combine. Chill for at least 1 hour before serving. Serve in individual glasses over ice. Garnish with remaining raspberries and mint leaves.

In our opinion, anything made with Campari can be classified as a stylish drink. It's so enticing, from the bottle with its turquoise label to the stunning old advertising posters to its still-secret recipe. This combination makes a wonderful aperitif.

clementine and campari

Campari 2 Tbsp (1 fl oz)

fresh clementine juice
2 Tbsp (1 fl oz)

Prosecco 6 Tbsp (3 fl oz)

clementine twist or wheel
for garnish

serves 1

Pour Campari into a chilled champagne flute. Top with clementine juice, then Prosecco. Garnish with a clementine twist or wheel and serve at once.

DARLING CLEMENTINES

Try to squeeze your own clementines for this cocktail, as their flavor is usually far superior to that of regular oranges. If you use oranges, Valencias are the ones to choose.

pom pom

fresh ginger ½-inch piece

fresh mint 6 leaves

lime ½, quartered

white rum 3 Tbsp (1½ fl oz)

pomegranate juice 3 Tbsp
(1½ fl oz)

Grand Marnier 1 Tbsp
(½ fl oz)

ice

ginger ale splash

pomegranate seeds
for garnish

serves 1

Slice ginger. In a cocktail shaker, muddle ginger, mint, lime, and rum. Add pomegranate juice and Grand Marnier and fill shaker with ice. Cover and shake well and strain into an old-fashioned glass filled with ice. Top with ginger ale and garnish with pomegranate seeds. Serve at once.

CHANGE IT UP

Thanks to the miraculous antioxidant powers of pomegranates, it's become easier to find the seeds, flown in from another hemisphere, outside of their dead-of-winter season. If you can't get them, mix this up with raspberries and raspberry juice instead.

Yuzu tastes like a combination of grapefruit and mandarin. Look for it in bottles in Asian markets; if you have trouble finding it, you can use any citrus juice as a substitute—the more exotic, the better.

orange blossom gin fizz

STIR IT UP

Another nice way to present this cocktail is with glass swizzle sticks. They make lovely tinkling sounds that seem just right for a garden party and they give guests something to do with their hands as they chat.

Fill a cocktail shaker with ice. Add gin, *yuzu* juice, orange wedges, orange flower water, and simple syrup. Cover, shake well, and strain into a highball glass filled with ice. Top with club soda. Garnish with an orange blossom (if using) and serve at once.

ice

gin ¼ cup (2 fl oz)

yuzu or fresh lemon juice 2 Tbsp (1 fl oz)

orange ¼, cut into 2 wedges

orange flower water ½ tsp

Simple Syrup (page 29) 1 Tbsp (½ fl oz)

club soda (soda water) ¼ cup (2 fl oz)

orange blossom for garnish (optional)

serves 1

moscato fruit punch

MULTICULTURAL MUSCAT

Muscat wine is made in an astonishing array of countries, from Italy to France to Serbia to Morocco. An Italian *moscato* is used here, but choose one that best echoes the origins of the dishes on your menu.

In a pitcher, combine the *moscato,* lemon juice, simple syrup, and mixed fruits. Stir well and pour into individual Collins or old-fashioned glasses filled with ice. Serve at once.

moscato 2 bottles (750 ml each)

fresh lemon juice ¼ cup (2 fl oz)

Simple Syrup (page 29) ¼ cup (2 fl oz)

mixed fruits such as peaches, apricots, and melon 2½ cups finely diced

ice

serves 6–8

seasonal sangria four ways

spring white sangria

fruity white wine such as Chenin Blanc or Gewürztraminer 1 bottle (750 ml)

passion fruit juice 1¼ cups

fresh lime juice ¼ cup (2 fl oz)

white and muscat grapes 1 cup each, seeded and halved

Asian or Bartlett pear 1, cored and thinly sliced

litchis 1 can (20 oz) with syrup

fresh mint and dill 2 Tbsp chopped each

ice

serves 6–8

In a pitcher, combine wine, passion fruit and lime juices, grapes, pear, litchis and syrup, mint, and dill. Stir well. Refrigerate until chilled and flavors have blended, about 2 hours. Pour sangria into individual Collins or old-fashioned glasses filled with ice for serving.

summer fruit rosé

Provençal rosé 1 bottle (750 ml)

white cranberry juice 1¼ cups

raspberries 1 pint

blackberries or cherries 1 pint

nectarine 1, pitted and thinly sliced

white peach 1, pitted and thinly sliced

ice

serves 6–8

In a pitcher, combine rosé, cranberry juice, raspberries, blackberries (if using cherries, be sure to pit them), nectarine, and peach. Stir well. Refrigerate until chilled and flavors have blended, about 2 hours. Pour sangria into individual Collins or old-fashioned glasses filled with ice for serving.

autumn fruit hard cider

Breton or other hard apple cider 1 bottle (750 ml)

ginger ale 1½ cups

Calvados ½ cup (4 fl oz)

fresh lemon juice ¼ cup (2 fl oz)

Ficelle or Bosc pears 2, cored and thinly sliced

red and green apples 1 each, cored and thinly sliced

cinnamon ¼ tsp ground, plus 6–8 sticks for garnish

ice

serves 6–8

In a pitcher, combine apple cider, ginger ale, Calvados, lemon juice, pears, red and green apples, and ground cinnamon. Stir well. Refrigerate until chilled and flavors have blended, about 2 hours. Pour sangria into individual Collins or old-fashioned glasses filled with ice for serving. Garnish with cinnamon sticks.

winter red sangria

fruity red wine such as Pinot Noir 2 bottles (750 ml each)

honey 3 Tbsp

red seedless grapes 1 cup, halved

oranges 2, thinly sliced

lemons 2, thinly sliced

Granny Smith apple 1, cored and diced

star anise pods 3

cinnamon stick 1

ice

serves 6–8

To make cold sangria, in a small saucepan, combine 1 cup wine with honey. Bring to a simmer over medium heat and stir to dissolve honey. Remove from heat and let cool. In a pitcher, combine wine-honey mixture with remaining ingredients. Stir well. Refrigerate until mixture is chilled and flavors have blended, about 2 hours. Pour sangria into individual Collins or old-fashioned glasses filled with ice for serving.

To make hot sangria, in a saucepan over medium heat, combine all ingredients, bring to a simmer, and stir to combine. Remove from heat and strain into heatproof mugs for serving.

The cosmo is an embellished descendant of the classic gimlet, made with lime juice and gin. It's also a kissing cousin of the vodka-based kamikaze and of another cranberry cooler, the Cape Codder. We love the aroma that elder flower lends to this riff on a perennial cocktail.

elder flower white cosmopolitan

ELEGANT ELDER FLOWER

We've found many uses for elder flower cordial, like adding a splash to Prosecco or using it to flavor *panna cotta*. It's fun to explore the lesser-known liqueurs and use them to round out your home bar.

Fill a cocktail shaker with ice. Add vodka, elder flower liqueur, white cranberry juice, and lemon juice. Cover, shake well, and strain into a chilled martini glass. Float a flower on top and serve at once.

ice

vodka ¼ cup (2 fl oz)

St-Germain elder flower liqueur 2 Tbsp (1 fl oz)

white cranberry juice 2 Tbsp (1 fl oz)

fresh lemon juice 1 Tbsp (½ fl oz)

edible flowers for garnish

serves 1

chinatown mule

CHANGE IT UP

For an even more exotic take on the classic Moscow mule, seek out Buddha's hand or another unusual citrus variety and use it in place of the lemon.

Slice ginger. In a cocktail shaker, muddle ginger, cilantro, brown sugar, and lemon zest. Add rice wine, vodka, lime juice, and enough ice to fill shaker. Cover, shake well, and strain into an old-fashioned glass filled with ice. Garnish with ginger slices, lemon zest strips, and lime slices. Serve at once.

fresh ginger ½-inch piece, plus thin slices for garnish

cilantro 3 sprigs

brown sugar 1 tsp

lemon zest ½-inch piece, plus strips for garnish

rice wine 6 Tbsp (3 fl oz)

citrus-flavored vodka 3 Tbsp (1½ fl oz)

fresh lime juice 1 Tbsp (½ fl oz), plus slices for garnish

ice

serves 1

simple syrup

....

sugar 1 cup
water 1 cup

makes 1½ cups

In a small saucepan, combine sugar and water. Bring to a boil over medium heat, stirring to dissolve sugar, about 3 minutes. Remove from heat and let cool. Store in an airtight container in refrigerator for up to 3 weeks.

rose syrup

....

sugar 1 cup
water 1 cup
rose water 2 tsp

makes 1½ cups

In a small saucepan, combine sugar and water. Bring to a boil over medium heat, stirring to dissolve sugar, about 3 minutes. Remove from heat and let cool. Add rose water and stir to combine. Store in an airtight container in refrigerator for up to 3 weeks.

Note: For a flavor variation, use 2 tsp orange flower water in place of rose water.

elder flower syrup

....

sugar 1 cup
water 1 cup
dried elder flowers 1 Tbsp or 1 tea bag

makes 1½ cups

In a small saucepan, combine sugar and water. Bring to a boil over medium heat, stirring to dissolve sugar, about 3 minutes. Remove from heat and add elder flowers. Let cool. Refrigerate overnight. Strain liquid through a fine-mesh sieve into an airtight container, and store in refrigerator for up to 3 weeks.

Note: For flavor variations, use 1 Tbsp or 1 tea bag of dried hibiscus or lavender flowers in place of elder flowers.

kaffir lime syrup

....

sugar 1 cup
water 1 cup
kaffir lime leaves 4

makes 1½ cups

In a small saucepan, combine sugar and water. Bring to a boil over medium heat, stirring to dissolve sugar, about 3 minutes. Remove from heat and add lime leaves. Let cool. Refrigerate overnight. Strain liquid through a fine-mesh sieve into an airtight container, and store in refrigerator for up to 3 weeks.

Note: For flavor variations, use a 2-inch piece of citrus peel or 1 lemongrass stalk, coarsely chopped, in place of kaffir lime leaves.

Who doesn't love a hot toddy? This version gains a lovely flavor and aroma from toasted sesame oil, used in place of butter. Here, we have also traded in the typical cinnamon, which can often be overpowering, for ginger and star anise.

spiced hot toddy

. . . .

COCKTAIL DRAMA

If you really want to put on a show, make each toddy the way Jamie's uncle did: heat a poker in the fireplace, combine the ingredients in a sturdy mug, and immerse the tip of the hot poker into the mug to warm up the toddy!

In a small saucepan over medium heat, combine apple juice, honey, ginger, and star anise. Bring to a simmer and stir to combine. Remove from heat. Add brandy and squeeze in juice from lemon half. Strain into a heatproof mug, reserving the star anise. Garnish with star anise and drizzle sesame oil on top. Serve at once.

apple juice ¾ cup (6 fl oz)

honey ½ tsp

fresh ginger ¼-inch piece

star anise pod 1

brandy ¼ cup (2 fl oz)

lemon ½

toasted sesame oil ¼ tsp

serves 1

cranberry fall warmer

. . . .

KEEPING WARM

Soothing and convivial, warm cocktails are intimate drinks, something we like to serve around the fire to close friends (preferably houseguests who are not driving home anytime soon after).

Using a vegetable peeler, remove a 3-inch piece of peel from the orange; reserve rest of orange for another use. In a small saucepan over medium-high heat, combine peel, cranberry juice, lemon juice, and honey. Bring to a simmer and stir to combine. Remove from heat and carefully pour into a heatproof mug. Add cinnamon stick and stir. Garnish with fresh cranberries.

orange 1

cranberry juice ¾ cup plus 2 Tbsp (7 fl oz)

fresh lemon juice 1 Tbsp (½ fl oz)

honey 1 tsp

cinnamon stick 1

fresh cranberries for garnish

serves 1

cherryade

. . . .

Bing or Rainier cherries 2½ cups, pitted

sugar ¼ cup

fresh thyme 1 sprig

fresh lime juice ¼ cup (2 fl oz)

ice

club soda (soda water) splash

serves 6–8

In a large saucepan over medium-high heat, combine cherries, sugar, thyme, and ¼ cup water. Cook, stirring occasionally, until cherries have softened, about 30 minutes. Remove from heat and let cool. Discard thyme, then transfer mixture to a blender and purée until smooth. Strain through a fine-mesh sieve into a pitcher. Stir in lime juice and chill for at least 30 minutes.

Fill individual Collins glasses with ice. Fill each glass one-third full with cherry mixture and top with club soda.

lemongrass green tea

. . . .

lemongrass 7–9 stalks

green tea 4 tea bags

agave nectar or honey ½ cup (4 fl oz), plus more if needed

fresh lemon juice ½ cup (4 fl oz)

ice

serves 6–8

Cut off and discard leafy tops from each lemongrass stalk, and trim off the bases of the pale, bulblike bottom parts. Finely chop 1 lemongrass stalk and set others aside for garnish. In a large saucepan, bring 6 cups water to a boil. Add tea bags, chopped lemongrass, and agave nectar. Remove from heat and let steep for 10 minutes. Strain through a fine-mesh sieve and let cool to room temperature. Once cooled, transfer to a pitcher, stir in lemon juice, and chill for at least 30 minutes. Taste and add more agave nectar if needed. Pour into individual glasses over ice. Garnish with lemongrass stalks and serve at once. You can add a sugar or salt rim (page 41) to glasses before filling them, if desired.

summer berry cooler

blackberries 1 pint

blueberries 1 pint

fresh mint ¼ cup
coarsely chopped

Lavender Syrup
(flavor variation,
page 29) 1 cup

fresh lemon juice
½ cup (4 fl oz)

ice

club soda (soda water)
4 cups

serves 6–8

In a pitcher, muddle berries and mint. Add lavender syrup and lemon juice and stir to combine. Fill pitcher three-quarters full with ice and top with club soda. Serve at once in individual glasses.

amalfi lemonade

lemon verbena leaves
8, plus leaves for garnish

sugar ½ cup

fresh lemon juice
1¼ cups

ice

lemons 2, thinly sliced

serves 6–8

Bring 2 cups water to a boil. In a heatproof measuring cup, combine boiling water with lemon verbena leaves. Stir in sugar to dissolve. Allow to steep for 10 minutes. Strain through a fine-mesh sieve and chill for at least 30 minutes. In a pitcher, combine lemon verbena syrup, 4 cups water, and lemon juice. Serve in individual glasses over ice. Garnish with lemon verbena leaves and lemon slices.

Light and sparkly, this grapefruit drink is a perfect way to kick off almost any dinner. The sorbet keeps the drink cold and looks beautiful (use a melon scooper for perfectly shaped little balls of sorbet). Serve the cocktail with a long spoon.

grapefruit fizz

· ·

grapefruit sorbet 3 small scoops

moscato 6 Tbsp (3 fl oz)

serves 1

Place sorbet in a chilled Champagne flute. Pour *moscato* carefully over sorbet and serve at once with a long spoon.

CHANGE IT UP

Of course, grapefruit is not the only choice. Experiment with other citrus and tropical sorbets to make your own signature fruit fizz.

champagne blush

· ·

Ice

Rose Syrup (page 29) 2 Tbsp (1 fl oz)

pomegranate liqueur 2 Tbsp (1 fl oz)

Champagne 6 Tbsp (3 fl oz)

serves 1

Fill a cocktail shaker with ice. Add rose syrup and pomegranate liqueur. Cover and shake well. Strain into a chilled Champagne flute and top with Champagne. Serve at once.

SERVE IT WITH

We think of this as a North African version of a Kir royale, and we often serve it with a meze platter, preceding a dinner of lamb kebabs from the grill.

fruity bellini three ways

bellini

superfine sugar ½ cup
(optional)

lemon 1, cut into
6 wedges (optional)

fruit purée of choice
(right and below)
¾ cup (6 fl oz)

Prosecco 2¼ cups
(18 fl oz/560 ml)

serves 6

If you choose to rim your Champagne flutes with sugar, pour a thin layer of sugar onto a small plate. Moisten outside rim of flute with a lemon wedge. Holding rim down at an angle, slowly rotate outside edge through sugar, taking care not to get sugar inside glass. Shake gently to remove any excess. Repeat with remaining flutes.

Add 2 Tbsp (1 fl oz) fruit purée to each prepared flute and top with 6 Tbsp (3 fl oz) Prosecco. If using sugared rims, be careful not to let Prosecco touch rims or it will fizz over. Serve at once.

white peach purée

white peaches 2
Simple Syrup (page 29)
3 Tbsp (1½ fl oz)

**makes about
1½ cups**

Peel, pit, and dice peaches. In a blender or food processor, combine peaches and simple syrup and purée until smooth. Taste and adjust flavor with more syrup as needed. Chill until ready to serve.

If desired, you can make purée in advance and freeze it in an ice-cube tray for up to 2 weeks, or up to 3 months if stored in an airtight container or resealable plastic bag.

mango purée

mangoes 2
Simple Syrup (page 29)
3 Tbsp (1½ fl oz)

**makes about
1½ cups**

Peel, pit, and dice mangoes. In a blender or food processor, combine mangoes and simple syrup and purée until smooth. Taste and adjust flavor with more syrup as needed. Chill until ready to serve.

If desired, you can make purée in advance and freeze it in an ice-cube tray for up to 2 weeks, or up to 3 months if stored in an airtight container or resealable plastic bag.

raspberry purée

raspberries 1 pint
Simple Syrup (page 29)
¼ cup (2 fl oz)

**makes about
1½ cups**

In a blender or food processor, combine raspberries and simple syrup and purée until smooth. Taste and adjust flavor with more syrup as needed.

Strain through a fine-mesh sieve, using the back of a large spoon to push fruit through. Chill until ready to serve.

If desired, you can make purée in advance and freeze it in an ice-cube tray for up to 2 weeks, or up to 3 months if stored in an airtight container or resealable plastic bag.

Our friend Larry Schwartz used to make Bloody Marys for the teachers at his university, and one day Worcestershire sauce wasn't available. Not one to give up easily, quick-thinking Larry used A1 steak sauce instead. Everyone loved it, and he went on to get excellent grades in school.

A1 bloody mary

CHANGE IT UP

If you're in a hurry for your hair of the dog, you can serve this with a skewer of olives in place of the pickled vegetables. Or, replace the horseradish with wasabi, drop in a Kumamoto oyster, and garnish with pickled ginger, and you have a Japanese-style oyster shooter.

To make pickled vegetables, trim radishes, carrots, haricots verts, wax beans, and okra. Cut celery into 4-inch lengths and cut radishes in half. Combine vinegar, sugar, salt, mustard seeds, star anise, and peppercorns in a small saucepan. Bring to a boil over high heat and stir to dissolve sugar. Place celery, radishes, carrots, haricots verts, wax beans, and okra in a large heatproof bowl. Pour hot vinegar mixture into bowl, making sure all vegetables are submerged. Let cool, tossing vegetables frequently. Cover and refrigerate for at least 2–4 hours before serving.

Squeeze the juice from the lemon halves into a large pitcher. Add tomato juice, horseradish, A1 sauce, celery salt, black pepper, cayenne pepper, and paprika, and stir until thoroughly combined.

Add vodka and stir to combine. Pour into old-fashioned glasses or tumblers filled with ice. Garnish with pickled vegetables and serve at once. Serve any remaining pickled vegetables alongside.

PICKLED VEGETABLES

French Breakfast radishes, baby carrots, haricots verts, wax beans, and okra ¼ lb each

celery 4 stalks

white wine vinegar 2 cups

sugar ½ cup

sea salt and yellow mustard seeds 2 tsp each

star anise pod 1, broken into pieces

peppercorns 6

lemon 1, halved

tomato juice 4 cups

horseradish 2 tsp freshly grated

A1 steak sauce or Worcestershire sauce 2 tsp

celery salt and ground black pepper 2 tsp each

cayenne pepper 1 tsp

paprika ½ tsp

vodka 2 cups

ice

serves 6

Using these sugar and salt rims, you can add another delicious textural element and flavor layer to your cocktails. They are visually appealing and feel good on your lips! Your guests will be very impressed.

rimming salts and sugars

. . . .

CINNAMON SUGAR

sugar ½ cup

ground cinnamon 2 tsp

CITRUS-INFUSED SUGAR

sugar ½ cup

lemon or lime ½

SMOKED SALT

kosher or sea salt ½ cup

smoked paprika 2 tsp

WASABI SALT

kosher or sea salt ½ cup

wasabi powder 2 tsp

makes enough to rim 4 glasses

To make cinnamon sugar, place sugar and ground cinnamon in a small bowl and stir until well combined.

To make citrus-infused sugar, place sugar in a glass jar or airtight container. Remove zest from lemon half in long, narrow strips and add to sugar. Stir until well combined. Tightly cover and let sit for at least 12 hours and up to 24 hours. Sift sugar through a fine-mesh sieve and discard zest strips.

To make smoked salt, place salt and paprika in a small bowl and stir until well combined.

To make wasabi salt, place salt and wasabi powder in a small bowl and stir until well combined.

To coat the rim of a glass, cover the surface of a small plate with a shallow layer of rimming salt or sugar (make sure plate is wider than glass rim). Moisten outside edge of glass rim with a wedge of citrus. Holding rim down at an angle, slowly rotate outside edge through coating ingredient, taking care not to get coating inside glass. Gently shake off any excess coating.

MIX AND MATCH

Many drinks beyond the margarita are enhanced by a salt rim. Try one on the A1 Bloody Mary (page 38) or the Cucumber and Chile Agua Fresca (page 18). A cinnamon-sugar rim is delightful with the Spiced Hot Toddy (page 30), and a citrus-infused sugar rim made with lime is perfect for the Ginger and Ginger (page 14). Interestingly, the Lillet Lemon (page 17) can stand up to sugar or salt.

starters

Starters and hors d'oeuvres can be playful and tactile as well as delicious. It's the only part of a meal that is regularly eaten with your hands in the Western world.

For these simple dishes, you need the best-quality ingredients. We recommend English Maldon sea salt. It has a great flavor and texture and, best of all, it's made in Maldon in Essex, which is close to where we're from!

grilled padrón peppers with sea salt

. . . .

HOW TO PRESENT

Delicious Padrón peppers are originally from the area around the town of the same name in Galicia, in northwest Spain. At casual dinners, we like to serve a heap of these addictive peppers, dusted with sea salt, on a rustic board.

Preheat a grill to high and oil grill rack. In a bowl, toss peppers with olive oil.

Grill peppers, turning occasionally with tongs, until skin has blistered on all sides, 3–4 minutes total. Season generously with salt and serve at once.

Padrón peppers 1 lb

extra-virgin olive oil 1 Tbsp

Maldon or other sea salt

serves 4

grilled asparagus with sea salt

. . . .

SERVE IT WITH

This is a perfect side dish and especially good with lamb or fish. Coupled with a dip, it also makes a great appetizer for a party. In spring, we grill a colorful mix of purple, green, and white asparagus and scatter lemon zest on top.

Preheat a grill to high and oil grill rack. In a bowl, gently toss asparagus spears with olive oil.

Grill asparagus, turning occasionally with tongs, until lightly browned but still crisp, 4–5 minutes total. Season generously with salt and serve with lemon wedges.

asparagus spears
1 lb, tough ends removed

extra-virgin olive oil 1 Tbsp

Maldon or other sea salt

lemon wedges for serving

serves 4

crudités

. . . .

small carrots such as Golden Nugget or mixed baby carrots ½ lb

French Breakfast radishes ½ lb

broccoli rabe ½ lb

tiny cherry tomatoes ½ lb

Lebanese or Persian cucumbers ½ lb, sliced on the diagonal

Treviso radicchio 1 head, leaves separated

choice of dips (*right and below*)

serves 4–6

Trim tops of carrots to 1 inch and halve lengthwise. Trim tops of radishes to 1 inch and halve lengthwise (keep whole if small). Trim bottom 3 inches off each broccoli rabe stem and discard.

Arrange all vegetables on a platter and serve with desired dips.

tzatziki

. . . .

English cucumber 1, peeled, halved, and seeded

lemon 1

plain whole-milk Greek yogurt 2 cups

fresh dill 2 Tbsp minced

fresh mint 2 Tbsp minced

salt and ground pepper

makes 2½ cups

Using the large holes of a box grater, coarsely grate cucumber. Place in a fine-mesh sieve and let stand at room temperature until most of liquid has drained out, about 10 minutes. Discard liquid and squeeze cucumber to remove any remaining moisture.

Grate zest from lemon into a bowl, then halve lemon and squeeze juice into bowl. Stir in cucumber, yogurt, dill, and mint. Season to taste with salt and pepper.

roasted eggplant dip

. . . .

eggplants 2, 1 lb total weight

lemon 1, halved

extra-virgin olive oil ¼ cup, or more as needed

garlic 1 tsp minced, or to taste

red pepper flakes ½ tsp

salt and ground pepper

feta cheese ¼ cup crumbled

fresh flat-leaf parsley 1 Tbsp chopped

makes 2½ cups

Preheat oven to 500°F. Pierce eggplants in several places. Roast, turning occasionally, until eggplants collapse and skin blackens, 15–30 minutes, depending on size. Remove from oven.

When eggplants are cool enough to handle, cut them open, scoop out flesh, and discard skin. Finely mince flesh and transfer to a bowl. Squeeze in lemon juice and add olive oil, garlic, and red pepper flakes. Season to taste with salt and pepper.

When cool, transfer to a food processor. Process until very smooth, adding a few teaspoons water or olive oil if necessary to achieve good dip consistency. Taste and adjust seasoning with salt, lemon juice, or garlic. Transfer to a serving dish, sprinkle with feta, and garnish with parsley.

our favorite hummus

. . . .

chickpeas 1 can (15 oz)

garlic 2 cloves

tahini ⅓ cup

extra-virgin olive oil ¼ cup plus 1 Tbsp

fresh lemon juice 2½ Tbsp

salt

fresh flat-leaf parsley 1½ tsp finely chopped

smoked paprika ⅛ tsp (optional)

makes 2½ cups

In a colander, rinse and drain chickpeas. Combine chickpeas and garlic in a food processor and purée until garlic is finely minced. Using a spatula, scrape down sides of bowl. Add tahini, ¼ cup water, ¼ cup olive oil, lemon juice, and ½ tsp salt. Purée until ingredients are combined but mixture is still semi-coarse.

Transfer hummus to a serving bowl. Drizzle with 1 Tbsp olive oil and top with parsley. Sprinkle with paprika (if using).

radishes with black salt and butter

....

assorted radishes such as Easter Egg, French Breakfast, and Cherry Bell 2 bunches

sea salts such as Hawaiian black and *fleur de sel* for serving

unsalted butter, preferably European style such as *Beurre d'Échiré or Celles sur Belles* for serving

serves 4–6

Clean and trim small radishes, leaving a few pretty leaves on top. Slice larger radishes in half.

Arrange radishes on 1 or more plates. Serve with salt and butter in separate small dishes or ramekins. Set out an extra bowl on the side for leftover radish tops.

A note on presentation
The classic way to serve radishes is with a small tub of soft butter and sea salt for sprinkling. Take advantage of all the wonderful varieties of European-style butter and of the various types of sea salt now available and offer more than one kind.

sliced watermelon radishes

....

large radishes such as Watermelon 6

sea salt such as Maldon, pink Australian, or *fleur de sel* for serving

unsalted butter, preferably European style for serving

serves 4–6

Clean and trim radishes. Using a mandoline, thinly slice radishes into round disks about 1/8 inch thick.

Arrange sliced radishes in a bowl. Serve with salt and butter in separate small dishes or ramekins.

A note on presentation
You can use other varieties of large radishes, such as Black Himalayan and Lime. When you have radishes in different colors and with variegated skin, slice them thinly to display the beauty of their interior.

french breakfast radishes on ice

French Breakfast
radishes
2–3 bunches

crushed ice

sea salt such as *fleur
de sel* for serving

unsalted butter,
preferably European
style for serving

serves 4–6

Clean and trim radishes, leaving a few
pretty leaves on top.

Fill a shallow bowl with crushed ice. Nestle
radishes in ice, keeping leafy tops visible.
Serve with salt and butter in separate small
dishes or ramekins. Set out an extra bowl
on the side for leftover radish tops.

A note on presentation
Radishes are best served ice-cold. If the
day is warm and you're dining outdoors, or
to add a simple touch of elegance anytime,
set the radishes on ice.

easter egg radishes with smoked salt

baby Easter Egg
radishes 2–3 bunches

sea salts such as
smoked and *fleur
de sel* for serving

unsalted butter,
preferably European
style for serving

serves 4–6

Clean and trim radishes.

Arrange radishes on 1 or more plates.
Serve with salt and butter in separate small
dishes or ramekins. Set out an extra bowl
on the side for leftover radish tops.

A note on presentation
Combine salts of different colors in a single
dish to show them off beautifully and create
visual impact.

grilled vegetables with romesco three ways

romesco sauce

plum tomato 1

garlic 2 cloves, crushed

Marcona almonds
1/3 cup

jarred roasted piquillo
peppers 1 cup, drained

red wine vinegar 2 Tbsp

day-old bread 1 slice

extra-virgin olive oil
1/4 cup

sea salt and ground
pepper

grilled vegetables
of choice (right
and below)

serves 4

In a food processor, combine tomato, garlic, almonds, piquillo peppers, vinegar, and bread and process until a rough paste forms, about 1 minute. Using a spatula, scrape down sides of bowl, then, with the motor running, gradually add olive oil until well combined. Season to taste with salt and pepper.

Transfer sauce to a bowl and serve with grilled vegetables.

grilled leeks

leeks 16 young, each
about 1/2 inch thick

extra-virgin olive oil
for brushing

sea salt and ground
pepper

Romesco Sauce (left)
for serving

serves 4

Using a paring knife, trim off root ends of leeks. Cut off tough green leaves and remove outermost layer of each leek. Make a 1-inch slit on both sides of each leek, cutting down to where white part of leek starts. In a large bowl of cold water, wash leeks thoroughly. Bring a large pot of water to a boil over high heat and blanch leeks for 5 minutes. Drain and pat dry.

Preheat a grill or stove-top grill pan to medium-high and oil lightly. Brush leeks with olive oil and season well with salt and pepper. Grill leeks, turning them with tongs every 2–3 minutes, until tender and nicely charred, about 8 minutes total.

Place leeks on a platter and serve with romesco sauce.

grilled escarole and radicchio

escarole 1 head

fresh thyme 2 sprigs,
finely chopped

extra-virgin olive oil
for drizzling

fresh lemon juice 1 Tbsp

sea salt and ground
pepper

radicchio 2 heads

Romesco Sauce
(above) for serving

serves 4

Split escarole lengthwise into quarters and pat dry. Scatter with half of thyme, drizzle with olive oil and half of lemon juice, and season generously with salt and pepper.

Cut radicchio lengthwise into quarters, being sure to keep some of stem attached to each quarter. Top quarters with remaining thyme, olive oil, and lemon juice, and season with salt and pepper.

Preheat a grill or stove-top grill pan to medium-high and oil lightly. Grill escarole until slightly wilted and charred on edges, about 5 minutes per side. Set aside. Grill radicchio until slightly charred, 3–5 minutes total. Place on a serving platter, drizzle with olive oil, and season to taste with salt and pepper. Serve with romesco sauce.

grilled summer vegetables

yellow summer squash,
zucchini, or a mixture
6 (3 lb total), halved
lengthwise

sea salt and ground
pepper

extra-virgin olive oil
2 Tbsp, plus more for
brushing

eggplants 4 small, thickly
sliced lengthwise

fresh lemon juice 2 Tbsp

Romesco Sauce
(above left) for serving

serves 4

Preheat a grill or stove-top grill pan to medium-high and oil lightly. Toss squash with 3/4 tsp salt, 1/2 tsp pepper, and 2 Tbsp olive oil. Brush eggplant slices on both sides with olive oil and season with salt and pepper.

Grill squash, turning once, until grill marks appear, about 6 minutes total (cover if using a gas grill). Move to an area with no coals underneath and grill, covered, until tender, about 4 minutes more. Grill eggplants, turning once and brushing with more oil if they look dry, until very tender, 6–8 minutes (cover if using a gas grill).

Transfer squash to a platter and drizzle with lemon juice. Arrange eggplants alongside. Serve with romesco sauce.

To be honest, we are a bit lazy when it comes to pasta. We think making ravioli at home is a pain. Wonton wrappers are the perfect solution. They're light and ideal for ravioli, tortellini, and small lasagnas. Look for them in supermarkets and Asian markets.

delicata squash ravioli

VARY THE FILLING

Use whatever type of pumpkin or squash you like. When we have some leftover roasted vegetables, we'll mix them with cheese and herbs and make these delicious ravioli.

Preheat oven to 375°F.

Cut squash into quarters, peel, seed, and cut into 1-inch chunks. Arrange on a rimmed baking sheet. Drizzle squash with ¼ cup olive oil and scatter garlic cloves and thyme sprigs on top. Season well with salt and pepper. Bake until tender when pierced with a fork, about 30–40 minutes. Remove and let cool.

Discard thyme and transfer squash and garlic to a bowl. Crush squash and garlic cloves with a fork until a rough paste forms. Stir in cheeses and season to taste with salt and pepper.

Arrange 6 wonton wrappers on a clean surface. Lightly brush edges of each wrapper with beaten egg, spoon 1½ Tbsp of squash mixture onto center of each wrapper, fold over into a triangle, and press edges to secure. Arrange filled wrappers on a baking sheet and cover with a damp kitchen towel to keep them from drying out. Repeat with remaining wrappers and filling. You should have 16 ravioli.

Bring a large pot of salted water to a boil. Meanwhile, heat 1 Tbsp olive oil in a sauté pan over medium heat, add spinach, and sauté until just wilted, about 2 minutes. Remove from heat. Add ravioli to pot of boiling water and cook until they rise to the surface and are semitranslucent, about 2 minutes. Carefully remove ravioli with a slotted spoon and add to pan with spinach. Gently toss over medium heat to warm, 1–2 minutes. Divide ravioli and spinach evenly among pasta bowls. Drizzle with remaining olive oil, top with walnuts and lemon zest, and serve at once.

Delicata squash 1 large, about 1½ lb

extra-virgin olive oil ¾ cup

garlic 4 cloves, crushed

fresh thyme 4 sprigs

sea salt and ground pepper

ricotta cheese ¼ cup

Parmesan cheese ½ cup freshly grated

square wonton wrappers 16

egg 1, beaten

baby spinach leaves 2 cups

walnuts ½ cup, toasted and chopped

lemon zest from 1 lemon, grated

serves 4

savory tart four ways

greek-style tomato and feta tart

....

puff pastry 1 sheet (½ package), thawed according to package directions

cherry tomatoes 1 cup, halved

ripe tomatoes 8, thinly sliced

feta cheese 6 oz, crumbled

fresh oregano 1 Tbsp chopped

sea salt and ground pepper

fresh thyme 6 sprigs

serves 4–6

Preheat oven to 400°F. Unfold pastry sheet on a lightly floured work surface. Roll out into a 9-by-13-inch rectangle about ⅛ inch thick. Cut in half lengthwise into 2 rectangles. Transfer rectangles to a rimmed baking sheet. Using a fork, prick each rectangle evenly over entire length. Fold in ½ inch of pastry along entire edge of each rectangle to create a border.

Arrange cherry tomato halves, sliced tomatoes, and feta cheese on top of pastry rectangles. Sprinkle with oregano, season with salt and pepper, and top with thyme sprigs. Bake until puffed and golden brown, about 20 minutes. Remove from oven, cut each tart into 4 pieces, and serve.

plum and goat cheese tart

....

puff pastry 1 sheet (½ package), thawed according to package directions

Santa Rosa or other small plums 6, thinly sliced

fresh goat cheese 6 oz, crumbled

lemon zest 1 Tbsp grated

extra-virgin olive oil for drizzling

serves 4–6

Preheat oven to 400°F. Roll out pastry sheet, cut in half, and shape border as directed (*left*).

Arrange plum slices on top of pastry rectangles and sprinkle with goat cheese and lemon zest. Bake until puffed and golden brown, about 20 minutes. Remove from oven and drizzle with olive oil. Cut each tart into 4 pieces and serve.

pear and gorgonzola tart

....

puff pastry 1 sheet (½ package), thawed according to package directions

pears 2, halved, cored, and thinly sliced

Gorgonzola cheese 6 oz, crumbled

walnuts 2 Tbsp chopped

fresh rosemary 1 Tbsp chopped

honey 2 Tbsp

serves 4–6

Preheat oven to 400°F. Roll out pastry sheet, cut in half, and shape border as directed (*above*).

Arrange pear slices on top of pastry rectangles and sprinkle with Gorgonzola, walnuts, and rosemary. Bake until puffed and golden brown, about 20 minutes. Remove from oven and drizzle with honey. Cut each tart into 4 pieces and serve.

leek, pancetta, and gruyère tart

....

olive oil 2 Tbsp

leeks 2, white and pale green parts, sliced into disks

pancetta 2 slices, coarsely chopped

puff pastry 1 sheet (½ package), thawed according to package directions

Gruyère cheese ½ cup shredded

serves 4–6

In a sauté pan over medium heat, warm 1 Tbsp oil. Add leeks and sauté until softened, about 2 minutes. Transfer to a plate and set aside. In the same pan over medium heat, warm remaining oil. Add pancetta and cook, stirring occasionally, until browned, about 5 minutes. Using a slotted spoon, transfer pancetta to a paper towel–lined plate and set aside.

Preheat oven to 400°F. Roll out pastry sheet, cut in half, and shape border as directed (*above left*).

Arrange leeks on top of pastry rectangles and sprinkle with Gruyère and pancetta. Bake until puffed and golden brown, about 20 minutes. Remove from oven, cut each tart into 4 pieces, and serve.

grilled figs with serrano ham

. . . .

fresh basil 12 small leaves, plus more for garnish

Black Mission figs 6, halved

serrano ham ¼ lb, thinly sliced

extra-virgin olive oil ¼ cup

sea salt and ground pepper

serves 4–6

Preheat a grill to medium-high and oil grill rack.

Place a basil leaf on cut side of each fig half, and wrap fig half with a slice of ham. Brush each fig parcel with olive oil. Grill until lightly marked, about 1 minute per side. Sprinkle with salt and pepper. Garnish with basil leaves and serve warm.

cantaloupe with bresaola

. . . .

cantaloupe 1, halved, seeded, peeled, and cut into 1-inch cubes

bresaola ½ lb, thinly sliced

fresh flat-leaf parsley ½ cup leaves

sea salt and ground pepper

serves 4–6

Using 36 short wooden skewers, thread a piece of cantaloupe, slice of *bresaola*, and parsley leaf onto each skewer. Arrange skewers on a platter, sprinkle with salt and pepper, and serve.

peaches, pluots, and coppa

....

peaches 4

Pluots or plums 4

coppa ½ lb, thinly sliced

sea salt and ground pepper

serves 4–6

Halve and pit peaches, and cut each half into 6 wedges. Halve and pit Pluots and cut each half into 4 wedges. Arrange peaches, Pluots, and *coppa* on a platter. Sprinkle with salt and pepper and serve.

grilled apricots with prosciutto

....

apricots 12, halved and pitted

extra-virgin olive oil ¼ cup

prosciutto ½ lb, thinly sliced

sea salt and ground pepper

fresh mint ¼ cup leaves

serves 4–6

Preheat a grill to medium-high and oil grill rack.

Brush apricot halves with olive oil. Grill, turning once, until lightly marked, 1–2 minutes per side.

Arrange 3 or 4 apricot halves on each individual plate. Divide prosciutto among plates and sprinkle with salt and pepper. Garnish with mint leaves and serve warm.

Fritto misto can be any combination of fish, meat (including offal), vegetables, or herbs. We love this seafood version: it's visually stunning, easy to serve, and just right for alfresco dining.

fritto misto

. . . .

CHANGE IT UP

If you have picky eaters at your party, you can substitute pieces of sole or haddock for any of the seafood. Sometimes we like to serve this in silver mint julep cups or glasses lined with parchment paper.

Pour oil into a wide, heavy saucepan to a depth of 3 or 4 inches and heat to 375°F on a deep-frying thermometer.

Meanwhile, in a large bowl, combine cornstarch and 2 Tbsp salt. Using your hands, toss squid, sardines, scallops, shrimp, and lemon slices in cornstarch mixture, making sure all are lightly and evenly coated.

Gently drop parsley into hot oil, turning carefully with a long-handled mesh strainer so that it cooks evenly. Fry until crisp, about 30 seconds. Remove with the strainer and drain on paper towels. Repeat this process with capers.

Make sure oil returns to 375°F. Working in batches to avoid crowding, remove a large handful of seafood and lemon slices from cornstarch, shaking off excess, and carefully drop into hot oil. Fry, turning them carefully with a wire skimmer so they cook evenly, until seafood is golden and floats to the top, 2–5 minutes, depending on size. Using the skimmer, transfer seafood and lemon slices to paper towels to drain. Repeat with remaining seafood and lemon slices. Transfer to paper towels to drain.

Arrange fried seafood and lemon slices on a platter and garnish with capers, parsley, and fresh lemon quarters. Serve at once, accompanied with aioli (if using).

vegetable oil for deep-frying

cornstarch 1½ cups

sea salt

squid 1 lb cleaned, bodies cut into 1-inch-wide rings and tentacles

small sardines 1 lb, cleaned

sea scallops ½ lb, preferably diver caught

medium shrimp ½ lb, preferably with heads on

lemons 1, thinly sliced, plus 4, quartered

fresh flat-leaf parsley 6–8 sprigs, washed and patted dry

capers ½ cup, patted dry

Aioli (page 175) for serving (optional)

serves 6

shrimp cocktail

lemon 1, halved

onion 1, quartered

kosher salt

bay leaf 1

black peppercorns 10

large shrimp 1½ lb

ketchup ½ cup

horseradish 1 Tbsp, prepared or fresh

lemon wedges for serving

serves 4–6

Squeeze juice from lemon halves into a pot filled with water, then add lemon halves, onion, 2 Tbsp salt, bay leaf, and peppercorns. Bring to a boil over high heat, then reduce heat to medium and simmer for 5 minutes to blend flavors. Add shrimp and cook until shrimp are opaque throughout, 2–3 minutes. Drain and let cool.

When shrimp are cool, peel but leave the tail segments intact. Using tip of a sharp knife, remove dark vein running along outside of shrimp. Put crushed ice on a large rimmed platter and pile cooked shrimp on top. In a small bowl, stir together ketchup and horseradish until combined. Serve shrimp with the cocktail sauce and lemon wedges on the side.

shrimp, crab, and avocado salad

cooked shrimp and fresh lump crabmeat ½ lb each

mango 1

extra-virgin olive oil, rice wine vinegar, and fresh lime juice ¼ cup each

cilantro ¼ cup minced, plus sprigs for garnish

jalapeño chile 1, minced

shallot 1, minced

sea salt and ground pepper

butter lettuce ½ head

avocado 1, diced

lime wedges for serving

serves 4–6

Peel and dice shrimp. Pick over crabmeat for shell fragments.

Peel, pit, and finely dice mango. In a bowl, stir together mango, olive oil, vinegar, lime juice, cilantro, jalapeño, and shallot. Season to taste with salt and pepper. Add shrimp and crabmeat and stir to combine.

Finely shred lettuce. In 4–6 clear glass tumblers, arrange lettuce in a layer on bottom. Top with crab mixture. Spoon avocado on top and garnish with lime wedges and cilantro sprigs. Serve at once.

crab and cucumber canapés

. . . .

fresh lump crabmeat
1 lb, picked over for shell
fragments

mayonnaise ¼ cup

celery 1 stalk, finely
diced

fresh chives 1 Tbsp
snipped

shallot 1, minced

fresh lemon juice
from ½ lemon

sea salt

English cucumber 1

paprika ¼ tsp

dill or fennel flowers
for garnish (optional)

serves 4–6

In a bowl, stir together crabmeat,
mayonnaise, celery, chives, shallot,
lemon juice, and salt to taste.

Slice cucumber thinly on the diagonal.
Place a dollop of crab mixture on top of
each cucumber slice, sprinkle with paprika,
and garnish with flowers (if using). Arrange
on a platter and serve at once.

shrimp and mâche salad

. . . .

Watermelon radish 1

plain yogurt ¼ cup

mayonnaise 3 Tbsp

Dijon mustard 4½ tsp

**grated lemon zest and
juice** from 1 lemon

fresh chives 2 Tbsp
snipped

shrimp ½ lb, cooked

fresh lump crabmeat
½ lb

mâche 6 oz

serves 4–6

Using a mandoline, thinly slice radish.
Set aside.

In a small bowl, whisk together yogurt,
mayonnaise, mustard, lemon zest and
juice, and chives to make a dressing.

Peel shrimp, leaving tail segments intact.
Pick over crabmeat for shell fragments.

Divide mâche among 4–6 salad plates
and top with an equal amount of shrimp,
crabmeat, and radish slices. Drizzle with
dressing and serve at once.

These are perfect appetizers for a family-style gathering or a big party. We served the shrimp one night at a get-together for fifty friends and everyone loved it! Put the seafood out on a large platter so your guests can keep diving in for more.

salt-and-pepper shrimp

Sichuan, pink, and black peppercorns 1 tsp mixed

shrimp in the shell 2 lb

sea salt

vegetable oil 2 Tbsp

garlic 4 cloves, minced

lemon wedges for serving

serves 6–8

Using a mortar and pestle, finely crush peppercorns.

In a bowl, combine shrimp, half of peppercorns, and 1 tsp salt and toss together. Set aside.

Heat a wok over high heat and add oil. Add garlic, remaining peppercorns, and 1 tsp salt and cook, stirring, for 1 minute. Add shrimp and cook until opaque throughout, 3–4 minutes. Serve at once with lemon wedges. Place a small bowl or dish on the side for discarded shells.

FRESH IS BEST

Here is another divinely simple dish where you need to use the very best of everything. Make sure you purchase high-quality shrimp. For a big party, we like to serve the shrimp on a board or large platter lined with waxed paper.

salt-and-pepper squid

baby squid 3 lb whole or 2 lb cleaned

black peppercorns ½ tsp

Sichuan peppercorns ½ tsp

sea salt

vegetable oil 2 Tbsp

green onions 2, thinly sliced

red pepper flakes ½ tsp (optional)

lemon wedges for serving

serves 6–8

If buying whole squid, clean (page 250), then cut bodies into rings ½ inch wide and bite-sized tentacles. If buying cleaned squid, cut up bodies and tentacles as described above.

Using a mortar and pestle, finely crush peppercorns. In a bowl, combine squid, peppercorn mixture, and 1 tsp salt and toss together. Set aside.

Heat a wok over high heat and add oil. Add squid and cook, stirring, until opaque throughout, 1–2 minutes. Transfer to a serving platter, toss with green onions, and sprinkle with red pepper flakes (if using). Serve at once with lemon wedges.

PARTY SERVICE

Sometimes we scoop this dish into paper cones, the perfect casual style for serving a crowd or an outdoor gathering.

Lobster says summer to us. This stylish little variation on the lobster roll is fantastic as an appetizer, but it is equally great for a picnic with your favorite potato chips! Just add a chilled bottle of rosé to the basket and you will be toting pure joy.

lobster sliders

VARY THE FILLING

We'll often make an assortment of sandwiches on tiny rolls for a picnic. Somehow their small size makes them more appealing. Other favorites are roast chicken breast with arugula on buns spread with herb butter, and mixed roasted vegetables on buns spread with aioli. You can vary the size, too. Use 4 standard brioche rolls and serve the sliders as a main course for 4.

To remove lobster meat, twist off claws from body. Using a lobster cracker or mallet, break shell on each claw and remove meat. Using a large, sharp knife, cut lobster in half lengthwise from head to tail. Discard black vein that runs length of body and small sand sac at base of head. Remove meat from body and tail. Twist off small legs where they join body to check for other chunks of meat. Chop lobster meat into ½-inch pieces.

In a bowl, combine lobster meat, mayonnaise, crème fraîche, celery, shallot, cornichons, tarragon, and lemon zest. Stir gently to blend and season to taste with salt and pepper. Refrigerate until ready to use.

Heat a large frying pan over medium heat. Butter cut sides of each roll. Place rolls, buttered side down, in pan and toast until lightly golden, about 1 minute. Transfer rolls to a work surface and spoon about 3 Tbsp lobster mixture on bottom half of each roll. Add a few leaves of Bibb lettuce. Top with remaining roll halves, secure with a toothpick if you like, and serve at once.

freshly cooked lobster 1 (2 lb total weight; about ½ lb meat)

mayonnaise 2 Tbsp

crème fraîche 2 Tbsp

celery 2 Tbsp finely chopped

shallot 1 Tbsp minced

cornichons 2, finely chopped

fresh tarragon 1½ tsp minced

lemon zest ½ tsp grated

sea salt and ground pepper

unsalted butter 1 Tbsp, at room temperature

brioche rolls 8 mini, split

Bibb lettuce 1 small head

serves 8

snapper ceviche

snapper fillet 1 lb, skinned

fresh lime juice ½ cup

fresh orange juice ½ cup

sea salt

red onion ½, thinly sliced

red jalapeño chile 1 small, thinly sliced

papaya ½, cut into ½-inch dice

extra-virgin olive oil 1 Tbsp

fresh flat-leaf parsley 1 Tbsp chopped

serves 4–6

Chill 4–6 small serving bowls.

Using a sharp knife, cut snapper into ½-inch pieces. In a large glass bowl, combine snapper with lime and orange juices. Sprinkle with salt. Chill, stirring occasionally, until fish turns opaque, about 50 minutes.

Drain off almost all liquid from fish. Return fish to bowl and stir in onion, chile, and papaya. Season to taste with salt and drizzle with olive oil.

To serve, divide ceviche evenly among chilled bowls and garnish with parsley.

yellowtail with avocado and basil

sushi-grade yellowtail fillet ½ lb

avocado 1, thinly sliced

extra-virgin olive oil 1 Tbsp

fresh lemon juice from 1 lemon

sea salt

fresh basil, preferably Thai 8 leaves, finely julienned

serves 4–6

Chill 4–6 serving plates.

Using a very sharp knife, trim away any sinew and skin from yellowtail fillet, then cut on the diagonal into slices ⅛ inch thick, allowing 6 slices per person.

To serve, arrange yellowtail and avocado slices on chilled plates and drizzle with olive oil and lemon juice. Season to taste with salt and garnish with basil.

tuna tartare with sesame

....

sushi-grade tuna fillet
¾ lb

fresh ginger ½ tsp
minced

**reduced-sodium soy
sauce** 1 Tbsp

toasted sesame oil
1 Tbsp

fresh lime juice 1½ tsp

jalapeño chile 1 small,
finely minced

fresh chives 1 Tbsp
snipped

black sesame seeds
1 Tbsp

serves 4–6

Chill 4–6 small serving bowls or glasses.

Using a very sharp knife, trim away any
sinew and skin from tuna fillet. Cut tuna
into ¼-inch pieces and place in a bowl.
Add ginger, soy sauce, sesame oil, lime
juice, and chile and stir to combine.

To serve, divide tuna among chilled bowls,
garnish with chives, and sprinkle with
sesame seeds.

wild salmon with lemon and mint

....

wild salmon fillet ½ lb,
skinned

lemons 2

extra-virgin olive oil
1 Tbsp

sea salt

red peppercorns ½ tsp,
crushed

fresh mint 1 Tbsp finely
julienned

serves 4–6

Chill 4–6 serving plates.

Using a very sharp knife, trim away any
sinew from salmon fillet, then cut on the
diagonal into slices ⅛ inch thick, allowing
6 slices per person.

Slice 1 lemon into paper-thin slices, and
juice remaining lemon. To serve, arrange
salmon slices on chilled plates, placing
lemon slices between the slices of fish.
Drizzle olive oil and lemon juice over
fish, season to taste with salt, sprinkle
with peppercorns, and garnish with mint.

croquetas three ways

ham and manchego croquetas

unsalted butter 4 Tbsp

garlic 1 clove, minced

flour 1 cup

milk 1 cup

sea salt and ground
pepper

Manchego cheese
1 cup grated

serrano ham ½ cup
minced

fresh chives 1 Tbsp
snipped

eggs 2, beaten

fresh bread crumbs
2 cups

canola oil 1 cup

makes 14 croquetas

In a saucepan over medium heat, melt butter. Add garlic and sauté until fragrant, about 1 minute. Add ½ cup flour and, using a wooden spoon, stir flour into butter until a ball forms. Slowly add milk, stirring constantly. Season with salt and pepper. Remove from heat and stir in cheese, ham, and chives. The mixture should be very thick. Transfer to a covered container and chill for at least 2 hours.

Lightly flour a work surface. Remove mixture from refrigerator and, using your palms, roll it into a log about 1 inch in diameter. Cut into pieces 2 inches long, and place on a lightly floured baking sheet.

Line a baking sheet with parchment paper. In 3 separate bowls, place ½ cup flour, beaten eggs, and bread crumbs. Working with 4 pieces at a time, place in flour and toss to coat, shaking off excess. Transfer to egg mixture and coat evenly. Finally, transfer to bread crumbs and toss to coat, again shaking off excess. Using your hands, roll croquetas into balls, or form into sausages. Place on prepared baking sheet, cover, and refrigerate until firm, about 30 minutes.

Preheat oven to 350°F. In a large sauté pan, heat oil over medium-high heat until shimmering. In batches to avoid crowding, fry croquetas, carefully turning once with a spatula, until golden, 3–4 minutes. Using a slotted spoon, transfer to paper towels to drain. Repeat with remaining croquetas. Return croquetas to baking sheet and bake until warmed through, about 3 minutes. Serve at once.

wild mushroom croquetas

Gruyère cheese 1 cup
finely grated

dried porcini
mushrooms 1 Tbsp finely
chopped

fresh flat-leaf parsley
1 Tbsp finely chopped

makes 14 croquetas

Prepare recipe as directed above, omitting ham and chives and substituting Gruyère cheese for Manchego. Stir in chopped porcini and parsley with cheese. Proceed as directed.

smoked paprika and ham croquetas

smoked paprika
1½ tsp

Fontina cheese 1 cup
finely shredded

makes 14 croquetas

Prepare recipe as directed above, stirring in paprika after sautéing the garlic and substituting Fontina cheese for Manchego. Proceed as directed.

catalan flatbread with three toppings

flatbread dough

active dry yeast
1 package (2½ tsp)

bread flour 2 cups
plus 3 Tbsp

warm water ¾ cup

sea salt ½ tsp

cornmeal 2 Tbsp

extra-virgin olive oil
for drizzling

topping of choice
(right and below)

makes 4 flatbreads

In a small bowl, stir yeast and ¼ cup flour into warm water. Let sit until foamy, about 5 minutes. In a food processor, combine remaining flour, salt, and yeast mixture. Process until mixture comes together in a dough, about 45 seconds. Transfer to a bowl, cover with plastic wrap, and let rise in a warm place for 1 hour.

Preheat oven to 450°F. On a lightly floured work surface, knead dough until smooth and springy, 5–8 minutes. Divide into 4 equal portions. Roll each portion into a ball with your hand. Roll out 1 ball into a strip about 2 by 10 inches. Prick evenly with a fork. Repeat with remaining balls of dough.

Transfer dough strips to 2 rimmed baking sheets sprinkled with cornmeal. Drizzle with olive oil, and finish with desired toppings.

tomato and goat cheese topping

flatbread dough (left)

cherry tomatoes 2 cups

fresh oregano 1 Tbsp
finely chopped

fresh goat cheese
5 oz, crumbled

**sea salt and ground
pepper**

makes 4 flatbreads

Prepare flatbread dough as directed. Bake flatbreads until crisp, about 8 minutes. Scatter tomatoes, oregano, and cheese evenly over top. Season with salt and pepper. Return to oven and bake until golden, about 3 minutes more. Remove from oven and serve at once.

radicchio and fontina topping

flatbread dough
(above)

radicchio 1 head

green olives 12, pitted
and roughly chopped

Fontina cheese ½ cup
coarsely shredded

**sea salt and ground
pepper**

extra-virgin olive oil
for drizzling

makes 4 flatbreads

Prepare flatbread dough as directed and set aside to rise.

Meanwhile, cut radicchio lengthwise into 8 pieces, being sure to keep some of the stem attached to each piece. Preheat a grill to medium-high and oil grill rack. Grill radicchio segments, turning once, until they wilt and are charred slightly, 1–2 minutes per side. Set aside.

Shape flatbreads as directed and bake until crisp, about 8 minutes. Scatter radicchio, olives, and cheese evenly over top. Return to oven and bake until lightly crisp, about 3 minutes more. Remove from oven, season with salt and pepper, and drizzle with olive oil. Serve at once.

prosciutto and arugula topping

flatbread dough
(above left)

prosciutto 6 oz, thinly
sliced

Parmesan cheese
2 cups shaved

arugula leaves 2 cups

**sea salt and ground
pepper**

extra-virgin olive oil
for drizzling

makes 4 flatbreads

Prepare flatbread dough as directed. Bake flatbreads until crisp and golden, 10–12 minutes. Remove from oven and scatter prosciutto, Parmesan, and arugula over top. Season with salt and pepper, drizzle with olive oil, and serve at once.

crostini four ways

avocado, basil, and tomato

French baguette 1 thin

extra-virgin olive oil
4 Tbsp

avocados 2

fresh lemon juice
from ½ lemon

heirloom baby
tomatoes 1 pint, halved

bush basil 4 sprigs

sea salt and ground
pepper

serves 8

Place an oven rack in upper third of oven
and preheat broiler.

To make crostini, cut bread on diagonal
into slices ¼ inch thick. Arrange slices on
a baking sheet and drizzle with 2 Tbsp
olive oil. Broil, turning once, until golden
brown, about 2 minutes per side.

In a bowl, combine avocados and lemon
juice and gently mash with a fork until
spreadable but still slightly chunky. Divide
avocado mixture evenly among crostini.
Top each with a few tomato halves and
a few basil leaves. Drizzle with 2 Tbsp
olive oil and sprinkle with salt and pepper.
Serve at once.

nectarine and prosciutto

crostini (left)

nectarines 4, halved and
pitted

prosciutto ½ lb, thinly
sliced

extra-virgin olive oil
2 Tbsp

sea salt and ground
pepper

serves 8

Prepare crostini as directed.

Using a mandoline, thinly slice nectarine
halves. Place alternating folded slices of
nectarine and prosciutto on each crostini.
Drizzle with olive oil and sprinkle with salt
and pepper. Serve at once.

fava, goat cheese, and mint

....

crostini *(far left)*

fava beans ½ lb, outer pods removed

fresh goat cheese 5 oz

fresh mint 2 Tbsp chopped, plus small leaves for garnish

fresh chives 1 Tbsp snipped

extra-virgin olive oil 2 Tbsp

sea salt and ground pepper

serves 8

Prepare crostini as directed.

Bring a pot of salted water to a boil over high heat. Meanwhile, prepare a large bowl of ice water. Blanch shucked fava beans in boiling water for 1 minute. Drain and transfer to bowl of ice water. When beans are cool, use your fingers to peel off their skin. Set aside.

In a small bowl, crumble goat cheese. Stir in mint and chives. Spread goat cheese gently over crostini and arrange a few beans on top of each. Drizzle with olive oil, sprinkle with salt and pepper, and garnish with a few mint leaves. Serve at once.

fig, gorgonzola, and arugula

....

crostini *(far left)*

Gorgonzola cheese ½ lb

figs 8, thinly sliced

baby arugula leaves ½ cup

extra-virgin olive oil 2 Tbsp

sea salt and ground pepper

serves 8

Prepare crostini as directed.

Spread Gorgonzola on each crostini. Top with a few slices of fig and some arugula. Drizzle with olive oil and sprinkle with salt and pepper. Serve at once.

chicken meatballs with ginger and lemongrass

ground chicken 1 lb

soy sauce 1 Tbsp

Asian fish sauce 1 Tbsp

lemongrass 1 Tbsp minced, white part only

cilantro 1 Tbsp chopped

fresh ginger ½ Tbsp grated

garlic 1 clove, minced

sea salt and ground pepper

grapeseed oil ¼ cup

lettuce leaves 14 small

green onions 4, thinly sliced

limes 2, cut into wedges

makes 14 meatballs

Preheat oven to 350°F. Lightly grease a baking sheet.

In a bowl, combine chicken, soy sauce, fish sauce, lemongrass, cilantro, ginger, and garlic. Season with salt and pepper and mix well. Roll into 1-inch balls and place on prepared baking sheet.

Heat a large frying pan over medium heat. Add oil and heat until shimmering. Add meatballs and panfry, turning balls to brown evenly on all sides, about 5 minutes total. Drain on paper towels. Return meatballs to baking sheet and bake until cooked through, 3–5 minutes. Season with salt and pepper.

Line a platter with lettuce and arrange warm meatballs on top. Garnish with green onions and limes.

CHANGE UP THE FLAVOR

These two meatball recipes highlight Asian and Spanish flavors, but our Greek-inspired meatballs are another favorite. We mix together ½ lb ground lamb; 1 garlic clove, minced; 1 Tbsp chopped fresh oregano; and ½ cup crumbled feta. For the sauce, we whirl in the blender ¼ cup each fresh mint and parsley, 1 garlic clove, ¼ cup walnuts, 1 anchovy fillet, and ½ cup olive oil.

spanish meatballs with chorizo and paprika

milk 2 Tbsp

stale bread ½ slice

fresh chorizo sausage and ground pork ½ lb each

fresh flat-leaf parsley 2 Tbsp chopped

sweet paprika 1 tsp

egg 1, beaten

sea salt and ground pepper

flour 2 Tbsp

extra-virgin olive oil ¼ cup, plus more for drizzling

makes 14 meatballs

Preheat oven to 350°F. Lightly grease a baking sheet.

In a bowl, pour milk over bread and allow bread to soften for 1 minute. Remove chorizo from its casing. In a bowl, combine milk-soaked bread, pork, chorizo, parsley, paprika, and egg. Season well with salt and pepper. Using your hands, mix until well combined. Roll into 1-inch balls, and dust balls with flour. Transfer to prepared baking sheet and set aside.

In a large frying pan, heat ¼ cup olive oil over medium heat. Add meatballs and panfry, turning balls to brown evenly on all sides, about 5 minutes total. Drain on paper towels. Return meatballs to baking sheet and bake until cooked through, 3–5 minutes. Season with salt and pepper.

Arrange warm meatballs on a platter and drizzle with olive oil. Serve at once with piquillo sauce *(right)*.

ON THE SIDE

Make a quick piquillo dipping sauce to serve alongside these meatballs. In a food processor, process ¼ cup jarred piquillo peppers and 1 garlic clove until a rough paste forms. With the motor running, gradually add ¼ cup olive oil until well combined. Transfer to a bowl and stir in ¼ cup chopped fresh flat-leaf parsley.

soups and salads

Once, in a restaurant, we were served soup in demitasse cups. We thought it was a lovely presentation, but we didn't have any demitasse cups at home. We did own gorgeous teacups, however, so we borrowed the idea from the restaurant and served soup in less-expected cups. We're always on the lookout for new ideas.

Here's our variation on a traditional Italian vegetable stew. The word *vignole* loosely means "a celebration of spring," so we like to throw in any spring vegetable we can find. It's also delicious with a spoonful of Salsa Verde (page 249) or a pesto (page 143) on top.

vignole soup

. . . .

PAIR IT WITH

This flavorful and brothy soup is delicious with a rustic, crusty bread, such as a baguette or a loaf of Pugliese. Or, pair it with savory crostini and a fruit dessert for a spring dinner. The soup begs for an Italian wine. Try a Sangiovese for an earthy red or a Vermentino for a bright and light white.

Trim artichokes (page 250), cutting each stem flush with bottom. Fill a saucepan three-fourths full of salted water. Add artichokes and thyme and bring to a boil over medium-high heat. Cook until artichokes are tender, about 10 minutes. Remove from heat and let cool in water. Drain and halve artichokes lengthwise. Using a paring knife, scrape away any furry choke. Set aside.

Bring a pot of salted water to a boil over high heat. Meanwhile, prepare a large bowl of ice water. Blanch shucked fava beans in boiling water for 1 minute. Drain and transfer to bowl of ice water. When beans are cool, use your fingers to peel off skins. Set aside with artichokes.

Cut leeks into 1-inch rounds and rinse well in cold water to remove any grit.

In a large saucepan over medium heat, warm olive oil. Add leeks, green onions, and prosciutto and sauté until prosciutto is lightly browned, about 3 minutes. Add chicken stock and bring to a boil. Add Swiss chard, sorrel, spinach, peas, artichokes, and fava beans. Simmer until vegetables are bright green and peas float to the top, 3–4 minutes.

Season to taste with salt and pepper, stir in mint leaves, and serve.

baby artichokes 8

fresh thyme 4 sprigs

fava beans 3 lb, outer pods removed

leeks 8 small, white and pale green parts

extra-virgin olive oil 2 Tbsp, plus more for drizzling

green onions 1 bunch, chopped

prosciutto 6 slices, torn into strips ½ inch wide

chicken stock 6 cups

Swiss chard 1 cup, shredded

sorrel leaves 1 cup, shredded

baby spinach leaves 1 cup

fresh or thawed frozen peas 1 cup

sea salt and ground pepper

fresh mint ½ cup packed leaves

serves 6–8

This is the perfect comfort soup, and it hits the spot on any occasion—after overindulging during the holidays, or when you feel like a clean, simple dinner with a few close friends. We like to squeeze in a fresh lemon wedge right before eating to brighten the flavor.

poached chicken soup with lemon and spinach

whole chicken 1, about 3½ lb

fresh ginger 1-inch piece, plus 2-inch piece, finely julienned, for garnish (optional)

onion 1, unpeeled, root end removed and halved

celery 2 stalks, quartered

carrots 2 large, quartered

fresh flat-leaf parsley handful of stems

fresh thyme 2 sprigs

black peppercorns 1 tsp

bay leaf 1 small

sea salt

baby spinach leaves 1 cup, coarsely chopped

lemon wedges 6–8

Sriracha chile garlic sauce 2 Tbsp

serves 6–8

Place chicken in a large stockpot. Add 1-inch piece of ginger, onion, celery, carrots, parsley, thyme, peppercorns, bay leaf, and 1 tsp salt. Fill pot with cold water to cover all ingredients by 2 inches. Bring to a boil over high heat and immediately reduce to a gentle simmer. Simmer, occasionally skimming any foam from surface, until juices run clear when you pierce thickest part of thigh, 1½ hours.

Remove chicken from pot and transfer to a plate. Let cool. Using a colander, strain stock, discarding solids. Line a fine-mesh sieve with two layers of cheesecloth. Strain stock through sieve to remove fat. Rinse pot and return strained stock to it.

Once chicken is cool enough to handle, use your fingers to remove and shred meat, discarding skin and bones. Add shredded meat to pot with stock and pour in any juices that have collected on plate. Season to taste with salt. Bring to a boil, add spinach, and stir just until wilted.

Turn off heat. Ladle soup into individual bowls and garnish with julienned ginger (if using). Serve at once with lemon wedges and Sriracha sauce.

SERVE IT WITH

Loaded with protein and greens, this soup is a one-pot meal. We like to serve it with a loaf of bread, a jug of wine, and a chocolaty dessert.

CHANGE IT UP

You can also stir in a peppery green like arugula or watercress in place of the spinach, or fresh pea shoots in spring. Check your local Asian market for all sorts of unusual greens to try in this soup.

watermelon with chile and lime

seedless watermelon
4 cups chunks

jalapeño chile 1 large

green onions 3, thinly
sliced

grated lime zest and
juice from 1 lime

fresh mint ½ cup packed
leaves, plus more for
garnish

rice vinegar 2 Tbsp

sea salt and ground
pepper

serves 4

Using a sharp knife, finely dice ¼ cup of
watermelon and set aside for garnish. Cut
8 thin slices from chile and set aside for
garnish. Seed and finely dice rest of chile.

In a large bowl, combine remaining
watermelon, diced chile, two-thirds of
green onions, lime zest and juice, mint,
and vinegar. Stir to combine.

Working in batches, transfer soup to
a blender and purée until smooth. Season
to taste with salt and pepper. Transfer to
a covered container and refrigerate until
cold, at least 1 hour. Ladle into chilled
bowls, garnish with reserved diced
watermelon and chile slices, remaining
green onions, and a few mint leaves,
and serve.

spring pea with mint

extra-virgin olive oil
2 Tbsp

shallots 2, minced

fresh peas 1 lb, shelled
and ½ cup blanched

vegetable stock 6 cups

fresh mint ¼ cup lightly
packed leaves

sea salt and ground
pepper

crème fraîche 6 tsp
(optional)

pea tendrils for garnish
(optional)

serves 6

In a large saucepan over medium heat,
heat olive oil. Add shallots and cook,
stirring, until softened but not colored,
2–3 minutes. Stir in unblanched peas and
sauté for 2 minutes. Add stock and bring
to a boil, then lower heat and simmer for
5 minutes. Remove from heat and let cool
slightly, then stir in mint leaves. Meanwhile,
prepare a large bowl of ice water.

Working in batches, transfer soup to a
blender and purée until smooth. Transfer
to a bowl and season to taste with salt and
pepper. Nestle bowl of soup in ice water to
cool, stirring occasionally. Once cool,
cover and chill until ready to serve. Ladle
into chilled cups and garnish with blanched
peas. Add crème fraîche and pea tendrils
(if using) and serve.

heirloom tomato with cucumber

English cucumber 1

ripe heirloom tomatoes 3 lb

green bell pepper 1

green onions 4, finely chopped

garlic 1 Tbsp minced

extra-virgin olive oil ⅓ cup

sherry vinegar 1 Tbsp

sea salt and ground pepper

vodka 1 Tbsp, chilled (optional)

Tabasco sauce

serves 6

Peel and coarsely chop cucumber, then coarsely chop tomatoes and bell pepper. Set aside 2 Tbsp each tomatoes, bell pepper, and cucumber plus 1 Tbsp finely chopped green onions for garnish. In a large bowl, combine remaining vegetables with garlic, olive oil, and vinegar. Season to taste with salt and pepper.

Working in batches, transfer soup to a blender and purée until smooth. Add vodka (if using) and pulse to combine. Taste and add more vodka if desired. Season again with salt and pepper. Transfer to a covered container and refrigerate until cold, at least 1 hour. Stir in Tabasco sauce to taste and serve in chilled glasses. Garnish with reserved tomatoes, green onions, bell pepper, and cucumber.

curried cauliflower with almonds

cauliflower 1 large head

extra-virgin olive oil 2 Tbsp

Granny Smith apple 1, peeled and thinly sliced

onion ½, finely chopped

Madras curry powder 2 Tbsp

vegetable stock 4 cups

milk 2 cups

Greek yogurt ½ cup

sliced almonds ½ cup, toasted

cilantro ¼ cup small sprigs (including blossoms, if available)

serves 8

Cut cauliflower into florets. In a large saucepan over medium heat, combine cauliflower, oil, apple, onion, and curry powder. Sauté for 5 minutes, cover, and steam for 5 minutes more, stirring often. Uncover, add stock, increase heat to high, and bring to a boil. Add milk and reduce heat to simmer gently for 10 minutes.

Meanwhile, prepare a large bowl of ice water. Transfer half of soup to a blender and add half of yogurt. Blend until smooth. Pour soup through a fine-mesh sieve into a bowl. Purée remaining soup and yogurt. Nestle bowl of soup in ice water to cool, stirring occasionally. Once cool, cover and chill until ready to serve. To serve, ladle into chilled cups and garnish with almonds and cilantro.

There are two main types of persimmon, Fuyu and Hachiya. We tend to use the sweeter Fuyus, which are still firm when they're ripe and can be cut very thin. Hachiyas must be quite soft before they can be eaten, making them difficult to slice.

endive salad with persimmon and pomegranate

. . . .

red or white Belgian endive 4 heads

pomegranate 1 large

ripe Fuyu persimmons 2

feta cheese ½ lb, crumbled

extra-virgin olive oil ½ tsp plus ½ cup

pistachio nuts ¾ cup, toasted and coarsely chopped

fresh chives 2 Tbsp snipped, tips and blossoms reserved for garnish (optional)

grated lemon zest and juice from 1 lemon

Champagne vinegar 1 tsp

sea salt and ground pepper

serves 4

Trim ends from endive, separate leaves, and place in a large bowl.

Seed pomegranate (page 250) and pat seeds dry. Using a mandoline, slice persimmons into thin slices.

In a small bowl, combine feta and ½ tsp olive oil and stir to combine. Add pomegranate, persimmons, feta, pistachios, and chives to endive leaves.

To make vinaigrette, in a small bowl, whisk together ½ cup olive oil, lemon zest and juice, and vinegar. Season to taste with salt and pepper.

Drizzle vinaigrette over salad and gently toss together. Season with additional salt and pepper, if necessary, and garnish with chive tips and blossoms (if using). Serve at once.

WHEN TO SERVE IT

We serve this crisp and refreshing salad in winter, when persimmons and pomegranates are in season. It pairs nicely with Spaghettini with Cauliflower Pesto (page 140) or Roasted Chicken with Spring Herbs (page 145).

CHANGE IT UP

Any salty or tangy cheese will do in this salad; try using fresh goat cheese or *ricotta salata* in place of the feta.

Of all the nutritious vegetables we should eat, beets are essential. At our house, we eat a lot of roasted beets. They're delicious on their own or tossed in salads. You can roast them a day ahead, let them cool in their skins, and then peel them when you're ready to serve them.

beet carpaccio

VARY THE PRESENTATION

Stacks for individual servings Slice beets ¼ inch thick. Stack 8 or 9 beet slices on each plate, and add cheese, vinaigrette, and garnishes.

Wedges for a party Keeping stem intact, cut each beet into 6–8 wedges. Arrange on a platter and drizzle with olive oil. Serve with cocktail picks and salt.

Family-style platter Slice beets ⅛ inch thick. Arrange slices in an overlapping pattern on a platter. Add vinaigrette and garnishes.

Cubes for starter salads Cut beets into ½-inch dice and transfer to a bowl. Add cheese, vinaigrette, and salt and pepper and toss to combine. Divide among plates or bowls and add garnishes.

Preheat oven to 400°F.

Trim off beet greens if still attached, leaving ½ inch of stems intact. Place beets on top of a large piece of foil. Drizzle with olive oil. Gather up edges of foil and seal tightly closed. Place foil packet on a rimmed baking sheet. Roast until beets are tender when pierced with a knife, 30–45 minutes. Remove from oven and unwrap beets.

When cool enough to handle, rub beets between paper towels to remove the skins. Follow 1 variation *(left)* to cut and plate beets, always cutting darker beets last to avoid staining lighter ones. Once beets are cut and arranged, add goat cheese (if using). Add vinaigrette (if using) and season to taste with salt and pepper. Garnish with mint, tarragon, and chervil and serve at once.

Candy Cane, golden, red, and/or white beets 8 mixed, in any combination

extra-virgin olive oil 2 Tbsp

fresh goat cheese 5 oz, crumbled (optional)

vinaigrette of choice (page 96) ½ cup (optional)

sea salt and ground pepper

fresh mint 1 Tbsp julienned

fresh tarragon 2 tsp coarsely chopped

fresh chervil 2 tsp leaves

serves 4–6

We're from England, and the Brits don't really go for watermelon. In fact, the only time Alison ate it as a child was while holidaying in Spain. Now that we live in the States, we love having it in our lives! These tangy, sweet salads are always a hit with our guests.

watermelon salad with purple basil and feta

seedless watermelon
1-inch-thick slice cut from
center (1–1½ lb)

Niçoise or Kalamata
olives 1 cup, pitted

feta cheese 5 oz, cut into
½-inch cubes

fresh purple basil ½ cup
lightly packed small leaves

extra-virgin olive oil ½ cup

fresh lemon juice from
1 lemon

sea salt and ground pepper

serves 4–6

Place watermelon slice on a cutting board and cut around outside to remove green skin and white flesh. Cut red flesh lengthwise and then crosswise, forming 1-inch cubes. Carefully slide watermelon onto a serving platter, taking care to keep shape of slice intact.

Sprinkle with olives, feta cubes, and basil leaves and drizzle with olive oil and lemon juice. Season to taste with salt and pepper and serve at once.

SERVE IT UP

We like to have fun with this salad. Sometimes we'll serve it in the watermelon rind itself. For a party, we give our guests tiny forks or toothpicks so they can serve themselves, bite by juicy bite—and sip a margarita or a cold beer while they're at it!

watermelon-jicama salad

jicama 1 small

seedless watermelon 3 cups
cubes

fresh lime juice 2 Tbsp

olive oil ¼ cup

wild arugula 1 cup

Marcona almonds 2 Tbsp,
coarsely chopped

ricotta salata cheese 5 oz,
thinly sliced

sea salt and ground pepper

serves 4

Peel jicama. Using a mandoline, cut into paper-thin slices. Transfer to a bowl, add watermelon cubes, and toss gently.

In a separate bowl, combine lime juice, olive oil, and arugula and toss to combine.

Divide watermelon and jicama evenly among 4 plates, or transfer to a large bowl for family-style serving. Top with arugula mixture, sprinkle with almonds and cheese, and season to taste with salt and pepper. Serve at once.

CHANGE IT UP

We prefer watermelon, but you can make these salads with cantaloupe or honeydew as well. Almost any melon, paired with salty cheese and spritzed with citrus, makes a fantastic and refreshing salad.

radicchio, spinach, and red sorrel

. . . .

radicchio 1 head, leaves torn

baby spinach leaves 4 cups

red sorrel leaves 1 cup

Blood Orange Vinaigrette (page 96) as needed

sea salt and ground pepper

serves 4–6

Combine radicchio, spinach, and sorrel in a serving bowl and toss with vinaigrette. Season to taste with salt and pepper. Serve at once.

butter lettuce with fresh herbs

. . . .

butter lettuce 2 heads, larger leaves torn, smaller leaves left whole

chives 2 Tbsp snipped, tips and blossoms reserved for garnish (optional)

fresh tarragon 2 Tbsp snipped

Champagne and Shallot Vinaigrette (page 96) as needed

sea salt and ground pepper

serves 4–6

Combine lettuce, chives, and tarragon in a serving bowl and toss with vinaigrette. Season to taste with salt and pepper. Garnish with chive blossoms (if using) and serve at once.

mâche, purslane, and green onion

·····································

mâche 4 cups

purslane 4 cups, thick stems removed

green onions 4, cut into 1-inch pieces (on the diagonal if thick)

Lemon and Thyme Vinaigrette (page 96) as needed

sea salt and ground pepper

serves 4–6

Combine mâche, purslane, and green onions in a serving bowl and toss with vinaigrette. Season to taste with salt and pepper. Serve at once.

arugula, oakleaf, and basil

·····································

arugula leaves 4 cups

spotted, red, or green oakleaf lettuce 4 cups

fresh purple or green basil ¼ cup leaves, larger leaves torn, smaller leaves left whole

Roasted Tomato and Basil Vinaigrette (page 96) as needed

sea salt and ground pepper

serves 4–6

Combine arugula, lettuce, and basil in a serving bowl and toss with vinaigrette. Season to taste with salt and pepper. Serve at once.

vinaigrette four ways

champagne and shallot vinaigrette

shallot 1, minced

extra-virgin olive oil
½ cup

Champagne or
Prosecco ¼ cup

Champagne vinegar
¼ cup

sea salt and ground
pepper

makes about 1 cup

In a small bowl, whisk together shallot, olive oil, Champagne, and vinegar. Season to taste with salt and pepper.

roasted tomato and basil vinaigrette

ripe cherry tomatoes
8, red or yellow

sea salt and ground
pepper

red wine vinegar ¼ cup

fresh basil 4 leaves

extra-virgin olive oil
½ cup

makes about 1 cup

Preheat oven to 400°F. Place tomatoes on a small rimmed baking sheet and season well with salt and pepper. Roast until skins are well blistered and burst, about 25 minutes. Pour vinegar over tomatoes and roast for 5 minutes more. Remove from oven and let cool completely.

Transfer roasted tomatoes and vinegar to a food processor and add basil and olive oil. Process until smooth, about 1 minute. Season to taste with salt and pepper.

blood orange vinaigrette

blood orange 1

extra-virgin olive oil
½ cup

red wine vinegar ¼ cup

sea salt and ground
pepper

makes about 1 cup

Cut off top and bottom of orange and stand it upright. Following contour of fruit, slice off peel and white pith. Holding orange over a bowl, cut along both sides of each segment to separate it from membrane, allowing it and any juices to fall into bowl. Using a fork, break up segments into bite-sized pieces. Add olive oil and vinegar and whisk until well combined. Season to taste with salt and pepper.

lemon and thyme vinaigrette

grated lemon zest and
juice from ½ lemon

extra-virgin olive oil
½ cup

white wine vinegar
¼ cup

fresh thyme 1½ tsp
leaves

sea salt and ground
pepper

makes about 1 cup

In a small bowl, whisk together lemon zest and juice, olive oil, vinegar, and thyme. Season to taste with salt and pepper.

bocconcini and toy box skewers

. . . .

**heirloom Toy Box or
cherry tomatoes** 1 lb,
red and yellow

fresh *bocconcini* 1 lb

fresh basil 1 cup leaves

**sea salt and ground
pepper**

red pepper flakes 1 tsp

extra-virgin olive oil
¼ cup

serves 4–6

Thread 3 tomatoes, 3 *bocconcini,* and
3 basil leaves onto a bamboo skewer,
alternating the ingredients. Repeat with
remaining ingredients; you should have
about 10 skewers. Arrange skewers on
a large platter and season with salt and
pepper. Sprinkle red pepper flakes on top
and drizzle with olive oil before serving.

heirloom fans with bufala

. . . .

heirloom tomatoes
4 large

**fresh mozzarella,
preferably *mozzarella
di bufala*** 2 lb, sliced into
¼-inch-thick rounds

fresh basil leaves from
½ bunch

**sea salt and ground
pepper**

extra-virgin olive oil
¼ cup

serves 4–6

Using a sharp knife, make a series of
lengthwise cuts into a tomato, spacing cuts
about ¼ inch apart and stopping about
¼ inch short of cutting all the way through.
Repeat with remaining 3 tomatoes. Tuck a
mozzarella slice and a basil leaf into each
incision. Arrange on a platter. Season with
salt and pepper and drizzle with olive oil
before serving.

baby tomato salad

. . . .

heirloom Toy Box, cherry, or pear tomatoes 1 lb

fresh *bocconcini* 1 lb, halved

sea salt and ground pepper

extra-virgin olive oil ¼ cup

fresh basil 10 leaves, finely julienned

serves 4–6

If tomatoes are 1 inch in diameter or larger, halve them using a serrated knife. In a large, shallow serving bowl, toss tomatoes with *bocconcini*. Season with salt and pepper. Drizzle with olive oil and sprinkle with basil before serving.

burrata with tomato wedges

. . . .

heirloom tomatoes 8 small

fresh *burrata* cheese 2 lb

sea salt and ground pepper

Lemon-Basil Pesto (page 143) ½ cup, or purchased basil pesto

extra-virgin olive oil ¼ cup

serves 4–6

Cut tomatoes into 1-inch wedges and arrange on a large platter. Cut open *burrata* to expose creamy center and place on platter. Drizzle tomatoes and *burrata* with pesto and olive oil and season with salt and pepper. Serve, instructing guests to scoop some cheese and tomato onto their plates.

Char-grilling squid is our favorite way of cooking these delicious (and fascinating) creatures. Did you know the squid uses precise jet propulsion to get about? We love the fresh and slightly spicy flavors in this Asian-inspired salad.

quick grilled squid salad

CHANGE IT UP

If you're not keen on squid or can't find it, this salad is also delicious with shrimp. Purchase 1 lb medium-sized shrimp; peel and devein them, then thread 4–6 on a skewer and grill them until they turn pink and curl up.

If buying whole squid, clean (page 250), then cut bodies into rings ½ inch wide and bite-sized tentacles. If buying cleaned squid, cut up bodies and tentacles as described above. In a bowl, toss squid with 2 Tbsp olive oil and season with salt and pepper.

Preheat a grill to medium-high and oil a grilling basket. Place squid rings and tentacles in basket and grill, turning once, until opaque and lightly charred on edges, about 1 minute per side.

In a bowl, whisk together 2 Tbsp olive oil, lime juice, mint, cilantro, and chiles. Toss squid with dressing and serve hot or at room temperature.

squid 1½ lb whole or 1 lb cleaned

extra-virgin olive oil 4 Tbsp

sea salt and ground pepper

fresh lime juice from 2 limes

fresh mint ¼ cup lightly packed leaves

cilantro ¼ cup coarsely chopped

Thai red chiles 2, seeded and minced

serves 4–6

If you find yourself stuck with hard, unripe mangoes, thinly slice them on a mandoline and use them in a fresh salad. They are delicious and have an almost sherbetlike flavor. Don't be afraid to serve this salad in the lobster shells. Your guests will love it!

lobster salad with green mango and mint

live lobsters 4, about 1¼ lb each

green mango or green papaya 1 large

black sesame seeds ½ tsp, toasted

white sesame seeds ½ tsp, toasted

fresh mint ¼ cup lightly packed leaves, torn or roughly chopped

fresh Thai basil ¼ cup lightly packed leaves, torn or roughly chopped

green onions 4, thinly sliced on the diagonal

grated lime zest and juice from 1 lime

Asian fish sauce 1½ tsp

sea salt and ground pepper

serves 4 as main course
serves 8 as appetizer

Bring a large pot of salted water to a rolling boil over high heat. Meanwhile, prepare a large bowl of ice water. Add lobsters to pot and boil, covered, for 12 minutes. Drain lobsters in a large colander and plunge into ice water. When lobsters are thoroughly cool, remove from bowl and let drain.

To remove lobster meat, working with 1 lobster at a time, twist off claws from body. Using a lobster cracker or mallet, break shell on each claw and remove meat. Using a large, sharp knife, cut lobster in half lengthwise from head to tail. Discard black vein that runs length of body and remove meat from body and tail. Chop tail meat into 4 pieces. Rinse carcass shell under cold running water, pat dry, and set aside.

Peel mango. Picture the pit inside, wide and flat, and use the tip of a knife to locate a flat side of the pit. These sides of a mango are fleshier. Using a mandoline, thinly slice a fleshy side of mango into paper-thin slices until you come within ½ inch of pit, then turn mango over and slice other fleshy side.

In a large bowl, toss together lobster, mango, black and white sesame seeds, mint, basil, green onions, lime zest and juice, and fish sauce. Season to taste with salt and pepper. Serve at once, spooning salad into reserved lobster shells.

SERVE IT UP

For a family-style meal, serve this salad in a shallow bowl, which shows off the ingredients and makes it easy for guests to serve themselves.

PAIR IT WITH

Lobster is always a special treat for us. When we do make it, we like to go all out and serve it with Champagne for a truly decadent meal.

smoked fish salad four ways

trout, watercress, and apple

smoked trout fillets ¾ lb

watercress 2 bunches, (about 3 cups tightly packed)

Fuji or Gala apples 2, halved, cored, and sliced ¼ inch thick

grapeseed oil ¼ cup

fresh lemon juice 2 Tbsp

lemon zest 2 tsp grated

serves 4–6

With a fork, flake trout into 1-inch pieces.

Trim coarse stem ends from watercress and separate into medium-sized sprigs.

In a bowl, toss together trout, watercress, and apples. Drizzle with grapeseed oil and lemon juice, sprinkle with lemon zest, and toss well. Transfer to a serving platter and serve at once.

salmon and fingerlings

fingerling potatoes 1 lb small

sea salt and ground pepper

crème fraîche ½ cup

horseradish 1 Tbsp prepared

lemon zest from 1 lemon, grated

fresh chives 2 Tbsp snipped, tips reserved for garnish

smoked salmon ½ lb, thinly sliced and torn into 1-inch strips

serves 4–6

In a saucepan, combine potatoes, 1 Tbsp salt, and water to cover by 2 inches. Place over high heat, bring to a boil, and boil until just knife-tender, about 10 minutes.

Drain potatoes and set aside until just cool enough to handle. Cut potatoes in half lengthwise and set aside in a bowl. Cover to keep warm.

In a bowl, combine crème fraîche, horseradish, lemon zest, and snipped chives. Stir to combine. Gently stir in potatoes and smoked salmon and season to taste with salt and pepper. Divide among individual plates, garnish with chive tips, and serve at once.

salmon, frisée, and poached egg

white wine vinegar and whole-grain mustard 1 Tbsp each

extra-virgin olive oil ¼ cup

sea salt and ground pepper

distilled vinegar 1 Tbsp

frisée 1 head

Croutons (page 249) 12

smoked salmon ½ lb, thinly sliced and torn into 1-inch strips

free-range eggs 4

chervil ¼ cup leaves

chives 1 Tbsp snipped

serves 4

In a bowl, combine white wine vinegar and mustard. Add oil in a slow stream, whisking constantly. Season to taste and set aside.

Half fill a sauté pan with water, bring to a simmer, and add distilled vinegar.

Meanwhile, tear frisée leaves into bite-sized pieces and toss with vinaigrette. Add croutons and smoked salmon. Divide salad among individual plates.

Working quickly, crack 1 egg into a teacup, then slide egg into simmering water. Repeat with remaining eggs. Poach until whites are no longer translucent, 3–4 minutes. Remove with a slotted spoon, pat undersides with a paper towel, and slide onto salads. Garnish with chervil and chives, season to taste with salt and pepper, and serve.

trout, cucumber, and dill

smoked trout fillets 1 lb

English cucumber 1, cut into 4 equal pieces

superfine capers ½ cup

fresh dill 2 Tbsp roughly chopped

fresh flat-leaf parsley ½ cup torn leaves

plain low-fat Greek yogurt ½ cup

red onion 1 small, minced

fresh lemon juice 1 Tbsp

extra-virgin olive oil ¼ cup

sea salt and ground pepper

serves 4–6

With a fork, flake trout into 1-inch pieces.

Using a mandoline, cut cucumber pieces into paper-thin slices. In a large bowl, combine cucumber slices, trout, capers, dill, and parsley.

In a small bowl, combine yogurt, onion, and lemon juice. Add oil in a slow stream, whisking constantly. Pour mixture over salad, season to taste with salt and pepper, and toss to combine. Transfer to a serving platter and serve at once.

In Japanese, *su* means vinegar and *mono* means thing. So this delicious dish literally translates to "vinegared thing." Pickled crab and cucumber salad is a healthy, simple favorite of ours, and we have hooked many friends, too.

crab sunomono

. . . .

cucumber 1 large English, or 2 or 3 Japanese

sea salt

fresh lump crabmeat ½ lb, picked over for shell fragments

seasoned rice vinegar ¼ cup

sake 1 Tbsp

sugar 1 tsp

reduced-sodium soy sauce 1 tsp

toasted sesame oil ¼ tsp

sesame seeds 1 tsp, toasted

serves 4

Using a mandoline, slice cucumber into very thin slices. Sprinkle cucumber slices with 1 tsp salt and toss to combine. Place in a fine-mesh sieve and let stand at room temperature until most of liquid has drained out, about 10 minutes. Discard liquid and squeeze cucumbers to remove any remaining moisture.

In a bowl, combine crabmeat and cucumber slices. In a separate small bowl, combine vinegar, sake, sugar, soy sauce, and sesame oil and whisk until well combined. Pour vinegar mixture over cucumber and crab mixture and toss to combine.

Divide crab mixture among individual plates and sprinkle with sesame seeds. Serve at once.

PAIR IT WITH

This dish is divine with sake (or any sake-based cocktail), but we also like serving it with a Japanese beer like Asahi or Sapporo.

CHANGE IT UP

We also like making this salad with daikon or raw asparagus, thinly sliced, in place of the cucumber.

charred orange, escarole, and almonds

....

Valencia oranges
4 large

extra-virgin olive oil
for drizzling, plus ¼ cup

escarole 1 head, tough
outer leaves removed and
leaves separated and torn

fresh flat-leaf parsley
¼ cup coarsely chopped

sherry vinegar 1 Tbsp

**sea salt and ground
pepper**

Marcona almonds
½ cup, coarsely chopped

serves 4

Preheat a grill or grill pan to high.

Using a sharp knife, cut off top and bottom
of oranges and stand upright. Following
the contour of fruit, slice off peel and
white pith. Cut oranges crosswise into
slices ¼ inch thick. Drizzle with olive oil.
Grill orange slices, turning once, until well
charred on both sides, 2–4 minutes total.
Set aside.

In a bowl, combine escarole, parsley,
¼ cup olive oil, and vinegar and toss to
coat. Season to taste with salt and pepper.
Add oranges and almonds, toss well, and
divide salad evenly among individual
plates. Serve at once.

pomelo, jicama, and chile

....

pomelo 1 large

jicama ½ small, peeled

green onions 4, thinly
sliced on the diagonal

Thai chile 1 small,
seeded and minced

pepitas **(pumpkin
seeds)** ½ cup toasted

cilantro 2 Tbsp coarsely
chopped

**sea salt and ground
pepper**

serves 4–6

Peel and segment pomelo (page 250),
letting each section and juices drop into
a bowl. Using a fork, break up segments
into bite-sized pieces.

Using a mandoline, cut jicama into paper-
thin slices. Add jicama to pomelo along
with green onions, chile, *pepitas*, and
cilantro. Stir to combine and season to taste
with salt and pepper. Serve at once.

grapefruit, avocado, and beet

. . . .

golden beets 2, trimmed

extra-virgin olive oil
2 Tbsp, plus more for
drizzling

pink grapefruits 2 large

Champagne vinegar
1½ tsp

Hass avocados 2, sliced

fresh basil ½ cup leaves,
torn

red onion ½, very thinly
sliced

**sea salt and ground
pepper**

serves 4

Preheat oven to 350°F. Coat beets with
2 Tbsp olive oil and wrap in foil. Place on
a rimmed baking sheet and roast until tender
when pierced with a knife, about 1 hour.
Remove from oven and unwrap. When cool
enough to handle, rub beets between paper
towels to remove skins. Set aside.

Peel and segment grapefruits (page 250),
letting segments and juices drop into
a bowl. Set aside.

Using a mandoline, slice beets into paper-
thin slices. Place beets in a bowl, drizzle
with oil and vinegar, and toss. Add
grapefruits, avocados, basil, and onion,
and season to taste with salt and pepper.

Divide among individual glasses or plates
and serve at once.

orange, mint, and hazelnut

. . . .

blood oranges 3

navel oranges 3

hazelnuts ¼ cup, toasted
and roughly chopped

extra-virgin olive oil
3 Tbsp

**sea salt and ground
pepper**

fresh mint leaves from
6 sprigs, torn if large

serves 4–6

Using a sharp knife, cut off top and bottom
of oranges and stand upright. Following
the contour of fruit, slice off peel and white
pith. Cut oranges crosswise into slices
¼ inch thick. Arrange on a platter. Scatter
with hazelnuts and drizzle with olive oil.
Season to taste with salt and pepper.
Garnish with mint and serve at once.

Asparagus is a member of the lily family, and can literally sprout up in one day. We always love eating the very first asparagus of the season and match it with fresh peas and lemon for a dish that's perfectly light, simple, and delicious.

pea and asparagus salad with meyer lemon dressing

DRESS IT UP

We use rice paper all the time. It can turn a loose dish, such as this salad, into something that's a little more special and easier to serve. Using a mix of asparagus—in this case green, white, and purple—makes for a very pretty bundle.

SERVE IT WITH

For a fabulous spring menu, we like to serve this salad with roasted lamb. And for dessert, our Sauternes and Lemon Honey Granita (page 222) adds an elegant touch, but Meringues (page 216) are also tasty and light.

Bring a saucepan three-fourths full of well-salted water to a boil. Meanwhile, prepare a large bowl of ice water. Add peas to boiling water and blanch for 1 minute. Using a wire skimmer, scoop out peas and refresh in bowl of ice water. Scoop out using skimmer and set aside.

Using the same water, cook asparagus until tender, 3 minutes. Drain asparagus and refresh in same bowl of ice water. Drain again and set aside.

In a bowl of hot tap water, soak rice paper sheets, 1 or 2 at a time, until they are pliable, about 30 seconds. Remove rice paper from water and cut each sheet into strips 2 inches wide.

Place 1 rice-paper strip on a dry surface and arrange 5 asparagus spears on one end (use fewer stalks if asparagus is large). Roll rice paper around asparagus to form bundle. Set aside and repeat with remaining rice-paper strips and asparagus.

In a bowl, combine peas, pea shoots, lemon zest and juice, and olive oil and toss to combine. Season to taste with salt and pepper. Transfer asparagus bundles to a platter or divide among individual plates, scatter the peas and pea shoots on top, and serve at once.

peas 2 cups (about 2 lb unshelled)

asparagus 2 lb, ends trimmed

rice paper 4 sheets

pea shoots 2 cups

shredded lemon zest and juice from 1 Meyer lemon

extra-virgin olive oil ¼ cup

sea salt and ground pepper

serves 6–8

We love artichokes and prepare them as much as possible. This is a great salad to have with a simple roasted chicken. The artichokes and beans can be cooked a day or two in advance and stored in their respective cooking liquids until ready to serve.

artichoke and cannellini bean salad

dried cannellini beans 1 cup, soaked overnight and rinsed in cold water

chicken stock 6 cups

fresh rosemary and thyme 4 sprigs each

garlic 4 cloves, crushed

sea salt and ground pepper

lemons 2, halved

artichokes 4 large

bay leaf 1

extra-virgin olive oil ½ cup

white wine vinegar 1 Tbsp

fresh chives 1 Tbsp snipped

white anchovy fillets 16, oil-packed

pecorino cheese 1 cup shaved

fresh flat-leaf parsley ½ cup leaves

serves 4

In a large saucepan, combine beans, stock, 2 rosemary sprigs, 2 thyme sprigs, and 2 garlic cloves. Season well with salt and pepper. Place over high heat and bring to a boil. Reduce heat to a simmer and cook until beans are tender, about 1 hour. Remove from heat and let cool in cooking liquid. When cooled, drain beans.

Meanwhile, fill a bowl with cold water and squeeze juice from 2 lemons into water. Working with 1 artichoke at a time, snap off tough outer leaves until you reach pale green inner leaves that form a cone. Cut off cone of leaves flush with where they meet bottom. Cut off stem to create a flat base. Then, with a vegetable peeler, trim off stringy layers where stem met bottom and where larger outer leaves were snapped off. As each artichoke bottom is trimmed, drop it in lemon water.

When all 4 artichokes are trimmed, drain, transfer to a saucepan, and cover with cold water. Add bay leaf, 2 rosemary sprigs, 2 thyme sprigs, 2 garlic cloves, and 1 tsp salt and place over high heat. Bring to a boil, then reduce heat to a simmer and cook until tender when pierced with a knife, 20–30 minutes. Remove from heat and let cool in cooking liquid.

In a large bowl, whisk together olive oil and vinegar. Add drained beans and chives to vinaigrette. Toss to combine and season to taste with salt and pepper.

Remove artichokes from cooking liquid and pat dry with paper towels. Using a teaspoon, scoop out furry choke from center of each artichoke bottom. Place each bottom on an individual plate. Top with bean mixture and scatter anchovies, pecorino, and parsley on top. Serve at once.

SERVE IT UP

We like to serve this salad atop the artichoke heart (the very best part), which makes for a dramatic presentation. You could also chop up the hearts, toss with the rest of the salad, and serve on its own or on a bed of greens, making it more of a salad.

shaved salad four ways

cabbage, pear, and ginger slaw

. . . .

seasoned rice vinegar ¼ cup

toasted sesame oil 1 Tbsp

fresh ginger 1 tsp grated

light brown sugar 1 tsp

soy sauce 1 tsp

napa cabbage ½ head

mango 1 firm, peeled

Asian pear 1, halved and cored

red serrano chile 1

sea salt and ground pepper

serves 4

In a small bowl, whisk together vinegar, sesame oil, ginger, sugar, and soy sauce. Set aside.

Using a mandoline, shave cabbage, mango, and pear into thin slices. Combine in a bowl. Cut chile into thin rings, remove seeds, and add rings to bowl. Add dressing and toss to combine. Season to taste with salt and pepper. Serve at once.

cucumber, red onion, and dill

. . . .

English cucumbers 2

red onion ½

fresh dill 3 Tbsp chopped

fresh mint 2 Tbsp chopped

rice vinegar 2 Tbsp

extra-virgin olive oil ¼ cup

sea salt and ground pepper

serves 4

Using a mandoline or potato peeler, shave cucumbers lengthwise into thin ribbons. Thinly slice onion. In a bowl, toss cucumbers and onion with dill, mint, vinegar, and olive oil. Season to taste with salt and pepper and serve at once.

squash, mint, and ricotta salata

. . . .

peas 2 cups

**mixed summer squashes
such as zucchini, yellow
squash, and pattypan**
1 lb

ricotta salata **cheese**
¼ lb, shaved

green onions 2, thinly
sliced on the diagonal

fresh mint ¼ cup
chopped

extra-virgin olive oil
¼ cup

**sea salt and ground
pepper**

serves 4

Bring a saucepan three-fourths full of well-salted water to a boil. Meanwhile, prepare a large bowl of ice water. Add peas to boiling water and blanch for 1 minute. Using a wire skimmer, scoop out peas and refresh in bowl of ice water. Scoop out using skimmer and set aside.

Using a mandoline or potato peeler, shave squash lengthwise into thin ribbons. In a bowl, toss together squash, peas, *ricotta salata*, green onions, mint, and olive oil. Season to taste with salt and pepper and serve at once.

carrots, olives, and almonds

. . . .

multicolored carrots
1 lb

green olives ¼ cup,
pitted

fresh flat-leaf parsley
¼ cup leaves lightly
packed

extra-virgin olive oil
2 Tbsp

fresh lemon juice 1 tsp

cumin seeds ½ tsp,
toasted

**sea salt and ground
pepper**

almonds ¼ cup, toasted
and crushed

serves 4

Using a firm-bristled brush, scrub carrots in a bowl of cold water. Drain and dry with paper towels. Using a mandoline, shave carrots lengthwise into thin ribbons. Set aside in a bowl.

Using a large knife, coarsely chop together olives and parsley. Transfer to a small bowl and add olive oil, lemon juice, and cumin seeds and stir to combine. Season to taste with salt and pepper.

Add olive mixture to carrots and toss well. Divide salad among individual plates or bowls, sprinkle with almonds, and serve at once.

We use a mandoline all the time. In fact, it's one of our favorite kitchen tools. It can transform the way you eat, salads in particular. Fennel, high in both vitamin C and fiber and low in calories, always makes us think of Italy. It's a staple in our cooking.

fennel salad with blood oranges and parmesan

. . . .

fennel bulb 1 large

blood oranges 2

Medjool dates ½ cup
coarsely chopped

extra-virgin olive oil
¼ cup

sea salt and ground pepper

Parmesan cheese 1 cup
shaved

serves 4

Trim fennel, peeling away any woody, fibrous outer layers and tough core and reserving fronds. Using a mandoline, cut fennel bulb into paper-thin slices. In a bowl, mix fennel slices with reserved fronds.

Peel and segment oranges (page 250), letting each segment and juices drop into a bowl. Add fennel, dates, olive oil, and salt and pepper to taste to orange segments and toss well to coat. Divide among individual plates, sprinkle with Parmesan, and serve at once.

SERVE IT WITH

This salad is tasty with almost any main dish. We serve it with roasted meats, pasta, or seafood. Or, we offer soup and crusty bread along with the salad and call it a meal.

fennel salad with apple, walnuts, and manchego

. . . .

fennel bulb 1 small

Granny Smith apples 2

celery 1 stalk

extra-virgin olive oil 3 Tbsp

white wine vinegar 1 Tbsp

walnuts ¼ cup, toasted and
chopped

sea salt and ground pepper

Manchego cheese ½ cup
shaved

serves 4

Trim fennel, peeling away any woody, fibrous outer layers and tough core and reserving fronds. Quarter and core apples. Using a mandoline, thinly slice fennel bulb, apples, and celery stalk.

In a bowl, whisk together olive oil and vinegar. Add fennel, apples, celery, walnuts, and salt and pepper to taste and toss to combine.

Divide salad evenly among individual plates, sprinkle with Manchego and reserved fennel fronds, and serve at once.

DRESS IT UP

For a fancy affair, we serve one of these salads as a plated starter. Other times, we might go for a big salad bowl and family-style grazing. By altering the presentation, you can make almost any dish fit any type of gathering.

The Jerusalem artichoke, or sunchoke, has had a bit of a rough ride in life. An old wives' tale linked it to leprosy, thanks to its resemblance to diseased fingers! And for years it was considered a poor man's vegetable. Sunchoke, we love you!

jerusalem artichoke salad with pomegranate and celery

WHEN TO SERVE IT

Bright and crunchy, this is a great salad anytime, but it is ideal for a winter menu. It's also quite pretty, adding fresh color to any dinner. We like to serve it alongside grilled or roasted meats, or even grilled kebabs (page 149).

Preheat oven to 375°F.

Peel Jerusalem artichokes and cut into ½-inch-thick slices. Place on a roasting pan, drizzle with 2 Tbsp olive oil, add thyme sprigs, season well with salt and pepper, and toss to coat with oil. Spread slices on roasting pan and roast, turning once, until golden, about 20 minutes. Set aside to cool.

Seed pomegranate (page 250), pat seeds dry, and set aside.

Using a mandoline, thinly slice celery stalks and place in a large bowl along with reserved leaves. Tear radicchio leaves in half and add to celery.

In a separate small bowl, whisk together ¼ cup olive oil and vinegar.

Add roasted Jerusalem artichokes to bowl with celery and radicchio and pour dressing on top. Season to taste with salt and pepper and toss to coat. Scatter *ricotta salata* and pomegranate seeds on top, and serve at once.

Jerusalem artichokes ½ lb

extra-virgin olive oil 2 Tbsp, plus ¼ cup

fresh thyme 2 sprigs

sea salt and ground pepper

pomegranate 1

celery 2 stalks, inner leaves reserved

radicchio 1 head, leaves separated

Champagne vinegar 1 Tbsp

ricotta salata **cheese** ½ cup crumbled

serves 4–6

mains

Our idea of a really great dinner is inviting six or eight good friends over and having a lovely bottle of wine, lamb chops roasted with lots of garlic, a nice vegetable gratin, and fresh green beans—that's the kind of food we crave.

Halibut, which grows very large, is a great fish to cook because it's firm and stays nice and juicy when panfried or roasted. Fennel is a natural choice for fish and when paired with citrus gets even better.

halibut with grapefruit, parsley, and fennel

CHANGE IT UP

We sometimes replace the fennel with shredded jicama, which is fresh tasting, crunchy, and a nice match for the citrus zing.

WAYS TO SERVE IT

You can serve this dish in different ways. Here are two possibilities: form a bed of the salad on the dinner plate and place the fish on top, or finely dice the salad and serve it as a salsa topping. This fish is also delicious with a polenta or root purée (page 196).

Peel and segment grapefruits (page 250), letting segments and any juices fall into a bowl. Add parsley to bowl and stir gently.

Trim fennel, peeling away any woody, fibrous outer layers and reserving fronds. Using a mandoline, cut fennel bulb into paper-thin slices. Add fennel slices and fronds to bowl.

Season fillets with salt and pepper. In a heavy frying pan over medium-high heat, warm olive oil. Add fillets and cook until browned on first side, 3–4 minutes. Turn and cook until opaque around edges, about 3 minutes longer.

To serve, transfer fillets to individual plates. Spoon grapefruit and fennel mixture on top, and drizzle with a little olive oil. Serve at once.

pink or Ruby grapefruits 4

fresh flat-leaf parsley 1 cup leaves

fennel bulb 1

halibut fillets 4, ½ lb each, skin and pin bones removed

sea salt and ground pepper

extra-virgin olive oil 1 Tbsp, plus more for drizzling

serves 4

Whole-roasted fish is one of Alison's favorite dishes to cook for friends. Filleting a whole fish is not too tricky, as long as the fish is properly cooked through, plus it allows for an impressive bit of tableside showmanship.

branzino with lemon and herbs

fresh flat-leaf parsley, thyme, and rosemary
4 sprigs each

garlic 2 cloves, thinly sliced

extra-virgin olive oil 2 Tbsp, plus more for drizzling

Mediterranean sea bass
2 whole, 1¼ lb each, cleaned, rinsed, and patted dry

sea salt and ground pepper

lemon 1, thinly sliced

serves 4

Preheat oven to 450°F. In a bowl, stir together herbs, garlic, and 2 Tbsp olive oil. With a sharp knife, cut slits on the diagonal 1 inch apart along length of both sides of each fish. Season fish inside and out with salt and pepper. Stuff cavities with herb mixture and lemon slices, dividing evenly. Place fish side by side on an oiled baking sheet.

Roast until fish flakes easily when prodded gently in slashes with a fork, 20–25 minutes. Transfer to a serving platter and drizzle with olive oil. To serve each fish, slide a sharp knife flat along backbone from base of head to tail. With aid of a serving fork, gently lift off top fillet. Lift off and discard backbone, leaving bottom fillet. Use a spoon to pull away any bones near head, tail, and along dorsal fin of bottom fillet.

FISH FACTS

Branzino is the Italian term for Mediterranean or European sea bass, not to be confused with Chilean sea bass or any number of other types of bass. You may find it sold under its Italian name or its French one, *loup de mer*.

snapper with olives and tomatoes

snapper 2 whole, about 1½ lb each

Gaeta olives 1 cup pitted

extra-virgin olive oil ¼ cup, plus more for drizzling

fresh thyme, oregano parsley, and mint
1 Tbsp minced each

garlic 1 clove, thinly sliced

tomatoes 2

sea salt and ground pepper

fennel bulb 1, thinly sliced

serves 4

Preheat oven to 400°F. Clean and rinse fish and pat dry. In a bowl, stir together olives, ¼ cup olive oil, thyme, oregano, parsley, mint, and garlic. Slice tomatoes ¼ inch thick. With a sharp knife, cut slits on the diagonal 1 inch apart along length of both sides of each fish. Stuff cavities with herb mixture, tomatoes, and fennel, dividing evenly. Place fish side by side on an oiled baking sheet.

Roast until fish flakes easily when prodded gently in slashes with a fork, 30–35 minutes. Transfer to a serving platter and drizzle with olive oil. To serve, fillet fish as described above.

CHANGE UP THE FLAVOR

As you can see from these two recipes, you can use a variety of ingredients to stuff and flavor a whole fish. Try ginger and green onion for an aromatic Asian twist.

seafood marinade four ways

lemon and herb marinade

extra-virgin olive oil
¼ cup

fresh thyme or dill 1 tsp
chopped

lemon zest 1 tsp grated

sea salt and ground
pepper

serves 4
(with four 6-oz fish fillets)

In a small bowl, stir together olive oil, thyme, and lemon zest. Season fish with salt and pepper. In a shallow dish, pour marinade over fish fillets, turn to coat, and let sit for 15 minutes before cooking.

saffron and coriander marinade

red onion 1 small,
thinly sliced

extra-virgin olive oil
¼ cup

coriander seeds 1 Tbsp,
crushed

lemon zest 1 tsp grated

saffron threads pinch,
crumbled

sea salt and ground
pepper

serves 4
(with four 6-oz fish fillets)

In a small bowl, stir together onion, olive oil, coriander seeds, lemon zest, and saffron. Season fish with salt and pepper. In a shallow dish, pour marinade over fish fillets, turn to coat, and let sit for 15 minutes before cooking.

fennel and orange marinade

extra-virgin olive oil
¼ cup

orange zest 1 Tbsp
grated

fresh or dried orange
slices 3

fennel seeds 1 Tbsp,
toasted

sea salt and ground
pepper

fennel fronds ¼ cup
roughly chopped

serves 4
(with four 6-oz fish fillets)

In a small bowl, stir together olive oil, orange zest, orange slices, and fennel seeds. Season fish with salt and pepper. In a shallow dish, pour marinade over fish fillets, turn to coat, and let sit for 15 minutes before cooking. Scatter fennel fronds over cooked fish just before serving.

soy-ginger marinade

reduced-sodium soy
sauce 3 Tbsp

fresh lemon juice
2 Tbsp

toasted sesame oil
1 Tbsp

fresh ginger 2 tsp
minced

star anise pods 2

sesame seeds 1 Tbsp,
toasted

serves 4
(with four 6-oz fish fillets)

In a small bowl, stir together soy sauce, lemon juice, sesame oil, ginger, and star anise. In a shallow dish, pour marinade over fish fillets, turn to coat, and let sit for 15 minutes before cooking. Sprinkle sesame seeds over cooked fish before serving.

Baking fish in paper is an all-around great technique: the fish steams in its own juices and whatever seasonings you've added, so it's low in fat and high in flavor, and it's a gentle way to handle the most delicate fish. And did we mention the cleanup is easy?

sole en papillote

PRESENTATION PANACHE

This simple preparation ensures a dramatic flair when served. As the pouches are opened at the table, the great aromatics of fennel and herbs release their fragrance, impressing your guests.

CHANGE UP THE FLAVOR

For a tasty flavor variation, swap out fennel for 2 cups baby spinach leaves, divided evenly among the pouches. Increase amount of parsley to 2 Tbsp chopped per pouch and substitute 1 Tbsp capers for the thyme. Proceed with recipe as described.

Preheat oven to 450°F. Cut 4 pieces of parchment paper, each 12 by 15 inches. Bring short sides of 1 sheet together, folding sheet in half, and crease. Unfold sheet and put a fillet to one side of crease. Season with salt and pepper. Top with 3 fennel slices, 2 lemon slices, and 1 sprig each thyme and parsley. Lay another fillet on top. Season again with salt and pepper and drizzle with 1½ tsp olive oil. Top with 2 more lemon slices, ¼ tsp fennel seeds, and 1 Tbsp fennel fronds. Bring uncovered side of parchment over fish and, starting at one end of crease, fold edges of parchment paper together in small overlapping triangles until package is completely sealed. Repeat with remaining ingredients to make 3 more packages.

Place pouches on a rimmed baking sheet and bake until puffed and golden, about 10 minutes. To serve, place each pouch on a dinner plate, and let dinner guests open their own servings.

sole fillets 8, 6 oz each, skin removed

sea salt and ground pepper

fennel 12 thin slices, plus 4 Tbsp roughly chopped fronds

lemon 16 thin slices

fresh thyme 4 sprigs

fresh flat-leaf parsley 4 sprigs

extra-virgin olive oil 2 Tbsp

fennel seeds 1 tsp, crushed

serves 4

This is a very simple method of getting the best out of your salmon. By keeping the fish fillet whole, it will stay moist in the oven, resulting in a juicy, fresh-tasting dish. Instead of serving it on individual plates, you can allow your guests to flake and serve it themselves.

slow-roasted salmon

wild salmon fillet 1, about 3 lb, with skin on and pin bones removed

extra-virgin olive oil 2 Tbsp

sea salt and ground pepper

fresh chives 1 Tbsp snipped

fresh chervil 1 Tbsp leaves

fresh flat-leaf parsley 1½ tsp minced

lemon wedges 8

serves 8

Preheat oven to 250°F. Line a rimmed baking sheet with foil.

Place salmon on rimmed baking sheet and rub all over with olive oil. Season well with salt and pepper. Place skin side down and allow to come to room temperature.

Bake until salmon is opaque on outside and there is no resistance when you pierce it with a skewer, 20–25 minutes. Let sit for 5 minutes before serving.

To serve, use a fork to flake warm salmon into chunks. Arrange on individual plates, sprinkle with chives, chervil, and parsley, and garnish with lemon wedges.

SERVE IT WITH

We always serve this salmon with warm new potatoes, crème fraîche, and capers. Skinny spring asparagus works well as an accompaniment, too.

mussels four ways

provençal mussels

unsalted butter 2 Tbsp

shallot 1, minced

garlic 2 cloves, minced

dry white wine ½ cup

heavy cream ¼ cup

mussels 1½ lb, scrubbed and debearded

fresh flat-leaf parsley 2 Tbsp chopped

fresh tarragon 1 Tbsp chopped

crusty bread for serving

serves 4

In a wok or large saucepan over medium heat, melt butter. Add shallot and garlic and sauté until fragrant, about 2 minutes. Add wine and cream and simmer until liquid thickens, 7–10 minutes. Raise heat to high, add mussels, and toss to combine. Cover and cook, stirring occasionally, until all mussels have opened, 3–5 minutes.

Using a slotted spoon, transfer mussels to 4 serving bowls, discarding any that failed to open. Ladle the liquid over the mussels, garnish with parsley and tarragon, and serve with bread.

mussels with saffron and tomatoes

extra-virgin olive oil 3 Tbsp

garlic 3 cloves, minced

red pepper flakes ½ tsp

canned diced tomatoes 1 cup, with juices

vermouth ½ cup

saffron threads pinch, toasted, ground, and dissolved in 1 Tbsp hot water

mussels 1½ lb, scrubbed and debearded

fresh basil ⅓ cup finely shredded leaves

crusty bread for serving

serves 4

In a wok or large saucepan over medium heat, warm olive oil until shimmering. Add garlic and red pepper flakes to taste and sauté until fragrant, 2 minutes. Add tomatoes with their juices, vermouth, and saffron. Raise heat to medium-high and simmer for 3 minutes to blend flavors. Raise heat to high, add mussels, and toss to combine. Cover and cook, stirring occasionally, until all mussels have opened, 3–5 minutes.

Using a slotted spoon, transfer mussels to 4 serving bowls, discarding any that failed to open. Ladle liquid over mussels, sprinkle with basil, and serve with bread.

thai green curry mussels

lemongrass 1 stalk

coconut milk 1 can (14 fl oz)

Thai green curry paste 1 Tbsp

Asian fish sauce 1 Tbsp

kaffir lime leaf 1

mussels 1½ lb, scrubbed and debearded

Thai chile 1 small, seeded and minced

cilantro 3 Tbsp chopped

crusty bread for serving

serves 4

Cut bottom third of lemongrass stalk into 1-inch pieces. Crush pieces with the flat side of a chef's knife.

In a wok or large saucepan over medium heat, warm coconut milk. Add lemongrass, curry paste, fish sauce, and lime leaf and simmer until fragrant, about 3 minutes. Raise heat to high, add mussels, and toss to combine. Cover and cook, stirring occasionally, until all mussels have opened, 3–5 minutes.

Using a slotted spoon, transfer mussels to 4 serving bowls, discarding any that failed to open. Ladle liquid over mussels, garnish with chile and cilantro, and serve with bread.

mussels with lemon and ale

unsalted butter 2 Tbsp

shallots 2, minced

sea salt and ground pepper

light Belgian-style ale 1 cup

mussels 1½ lb, scrubbed and debearded

lemon zest 2 tsp grated

heavy cream ¼ cup

fresh flat-leaf parsley 1 Tbsp finely chopped

crusty bread for serving

serves 4

In a large pot over medium heat, melt butter. Add shallots and sauté until fragrant, 2–3 minutes. Season with salt and pepper. Raise heat to high, add ale and mussels, and toss to combine. Cover and cook, stirring occasionally, until all mussels have opened, 3–5 minutes.

Using a slotted spoon, transfer mussels to 4 serving bowls, discarding any that failed to open. Stir lemon zest and cream into cooking liquid and simmer until liquid thickens, about 5 minutes. Ladle liquid over mussels, garnish with parsley, and serve with bread.

grilled scallops with salmoriglio

garlic 2 cloves, minced

lemon zest ½ tsp grated

fresh lemon juice ¼ cup

extra-virgin olive oil
¼ cup, plus more for
brushing

fresh oregano 2 tsp
minced

sea scallops 40

sea salt and ground
pepper

fresh flat-leaf parsley
1 tsp minced

serves 6–8

Preheat a grill to medium-high and oil grill rack. If grill has wide grates, use a grill basket.

In a small bowl, combine garlic with lemon zest and juice. Whisking constantly, add ¼ cup olive oil in a slow, steady stream. Add oregano and stir gently to combine.

Rinse scallops and dry well using paper towels. Brush scallops on both sides with olive oil and season well with salt and pepper. Grill scallops, turning once, until nicely charred, 1–2 minutes per side.

Arrange scallops on a serving platter and spoon sauce on top. Garnish with parsley and serve at once.

lemongrass shrimp skewers

large shrimp 36

fresh lime juice 2 Tbsp

Asian fish sauce 1 Tbsp

brown sugar 1 Tbsp

red chile 1 small, seeded
and finely chopped

lemongrass 1 Tbsp finely
chopped (white part only),
plus 12 stalks (optional)

cilantro ¼ cup chopped
(optional)

serves 6

Peel shrimp, leaving tail segments intact, and devein. In a small bowl, whisk together lime juice, fish sauce, brown sugar, chile, and chopped lemongrass. Put marinade in a resealable plastic bag and add shrimp. Seal and turn bag to coat shrimp. Marinate for 30 minutes.

Remove tough outer leaves of lemongrass stalks and trim stalks to 6-inch lengths to use as skewers. (Or, use 6-inch bamboo skewers.) Soak skewers in cold water for 30 minutes.

Preheat a grill to medium-high and oil grill rack. Thread 3 shrimp onto each skewer. Place skewers on grill and grill, turning once, until charred in spots, 2–3 minutes total. Garnish with cilantro (if using) and serve at once.

citrus-soaked squid kebabs

. . . .

squid 6, each about ½ lb, cleaned

sea salt and ground pepper

pomelo 1 large

fresh mint ½ cup torn leaves

red onion ½, thinly sliced

Thai red chile 1 small, seeded and finely chopped

serves 4

Soak 12–16 wooden skewers in water. Preheat a grill to high and oil grill rack.

Using a sharp knife, cut through one side of squid, then open it out flat. Score flesh in a crisscross fashion. Cut squid into bite-sized pieces and thread pieces onto soaked skewers. Season well with salt and pepper and set aside.

Using a sharp knife, peel and segment pomelo (page 250), letting sections drop into a bowl. Break into bite-sized pieces. Add mint, red onion, and chile and toss well. Season to taste with salt and pepper.

Grill squid, turning once, until nicely charred, 1–2 minutes. Arrange kebabs on a platter, spoon pomelo mixture on top, and serve.

pepper-crusted tuna kebabs

. . . .

mixed peppercorns 3 Tbsp

sea salt 1 Tbsp

paprika 1 tsp

sushi-grade tuna loin 2 lb

extra-virgin olive oil ½ cup

lemons 2, cut into wedges

serves 4–6

Preheat a grill to high. Finely grind peppercorns in a spice grinder.

In a bowl, combine ground pepper, salt, and paprika. Place tuna loin on a cutting board and cut into pieces about 1½ inches thick and 4–5 inches long. Roll each piece in spice mixture and set on a plate.

Drizzle spice-crusted tuna with half of olive oil and place on grill. Grill, turning to brown on all sides, about 4 minutes total for medium-rare. Let tuna rest on a cutting board for a couple of minutes, then cut each piece into 4 equal cubes. Lay the cubes in a straight line, cut side up. Thread a skewer through the center of each set of 3–4 cubes. Transfer to a serving platter, drizzle with remaining olive oil, and serve with lemon wedges.

This is a great and simple pasta dish and is really all about the quality of your shellfish. Be sure to use fresh, plump clams and mussels. We like to use Prince Edward Island (P.E.I.) mussels from Canada whenever possible, paired with small, juicy manila clams.

seafood linguine with leeks, fennel, and lemon

mussels ½ lb

manila or cherrystone clams ½ lb

leek 1 large, white and pale green parts only, rinsed

fennel bulb 1 small

linguine 1 lb

extra-virgin olive oil 4 Tbsp

grated lemon zest and juice from 1 lemon

sea salt and ground pepper

serves 4–6

Bring a large pot of salted water to a boil. Meanwhile, scrub mussels and clams under cold water. Discard any that are chipped or do not close when tapped, and debeard if necessary.

Slice leek into thin rings and separate. Trim fennel bulb, chopping and reserving fronds for garnish. Use a mandoline to thinly slice fennel.

When water reaches a rapid boil, add linguine and cook, stirring occasionally to prevent sticking, until pasta is al dente, according to package directions.

While pasta is cooking, heat a large sauté pan over medium heat. When pan is hot, add 2 Tbsp olive oil. Add leeks and cook, stirring, until just beginning to soften, about 2 minutes. Add mussels, clams, fennel, lemon juice, ½ tsp salt, and ½ tsp pepper. Cover pan and steam until shellfish have opened, 3–5 minutes. Discard any that do not open.

Drain linguine and add to sauté pan at once. Toss linguine with seafood to combine thoroughly. Transfer to a serving platter or individual shallow bowls. Drizzle with 2 Tbsp olive oil and garnish with fennel fronds and lemon zest. Serve at once.

SERVE IT WITH

We love to serve a big bowl of seafood pasta with a loaf of crusty bread, a simple green salad with Jamie's Lemon and Thyme Vinaigrette (Alison's favorite, page 96), and a Vernaccia or Sauvignon Blanc. Like the Italians, we never put Parmesan on seafood pasta.

CHANGE IT UP

If you're not a fan of mussels or clams, don't despair. You can make this linguine with crab or shrimp, too. Just use the same total amount—about 1 lb—of seafood.

This pesto is probably unlike any other you have tried. Poor cauliflower too often gets boiled, or slathered with cheese and broiled. Here, we've elevated it to a much higher and more dignified level. Charring it brings out a delicious nutty flavor that works perfectly with pasta.

spaghettini with cauliflower pesto

PESTO VARIATIONS

There are loads of different pestos to try, so get creative with your pasta toppings. We've included four more ideas (page 143) that make the most of seasonal ingredients. You simply can't go wrong serving pesto with spaghettini or linguine.

DRESS IT UP

Sometimes we like to serve pasta as a plated dish, rather than family style. We'll put a scoop of noodles in a shallow bowl, place the pasta bowl on a bigger dinner plate or charger, then add salad on the side. It's a neat and stylish way to present the meal.

Preheat a stove-top grill pan over high heat.

Season cauliflower florets with salt and pepper. Place on grill pan and cook, turning occasionally, until well charred on all sides, 6–8 minutes. Transfer cauliflower to a food processor and add olive oil, parsley, almonds, capers, and garlic. Pulse until mixture is well combined but still coarse. Set aside.

Bring a large pot of salted water to a boil. Add spaghettini and cook, stirring occasionally to prevent sticking, until pasta is al dente, according to package directions. Drain and transfer to a serving bowl. Toss with cauliflower pesto and Parmesan. Serve at once.

cauliflower 1 small head, cored and cut into 1-inch florets

sea salt and ground pepper

extra-virgin olive oil 1 cup

fresh flat-leaf parsley 1 cup leaves

almonds ½ cup, toasted

capers 2 Tbsp

garlic 2 cloves, minced

spaghettini 1 lb

Parmesan cheese 1 cup shaved

serves 4–6

pesto four ways

lemon-basil pesto

fresh basil 2 cups leaves
(1 bunch)

Parmesan cheese
6 Tbsp freshly grated

pine nuts 2 Tbsp, toasted

garlic 2 cloves, smashed

extra-virgin olive oil
6 Tbsp

**sea salt and ground
pepper**

**grated lemon zest and
juice** from 2 lemons

serves 4–6
(with 1 lb pasta)

In a blender or food processor, combine basil, Parmesan, pine nuts, and garlic and pulse until finely chopped. With machine running, drizzle in olive oil and purée until smooth. Season to taste with salt and pepper. Stir in lemon zest and juice. Alternatively, using a mortar and pestle, grind together pine nuts, garlic, and lemon zest until a thick paste forms. Add basil and continue to grind until smooth. Transfer to a larger bowl and stir in olive oil, lemon juice, and Parmesan. Season to taste with salt and pepper.

Use at once, or cover with plastic wrap, pressing it onto surface, and refrigerate for up to 1 week.

shiitake mushroom pesto

extra-virgin olive oil
5 Tbsp

shiitake mushrooms
10 oz, finely chopped
in a food processor

garlic 1 clove, minced

**sea salt and ground
pepper**

Worcestershire sauce
1 Tbsp

medium-dry sherry
1 Tbsp (optional)

pine nuts ¼ cup, toasted

Parmesan cheese ¼ cup
freshly grated

fresh flat-leaf parsley
½ cup packed leaves

serves 4–6
(with 1 lb pasta)

In a 10- to 12-inch nonstick frying pan over medium-high heat, warm 2 Tbsp olive oil until shimmering. Add mushrooms, garlic, and salt and pepper to taste. Sauté until mushrooms are golden brown and their liquid has evaporated, about 10 minutes. Add Worcestershire sauce and sherry (if using). Taste and adjust seasoning.

Transfer to a food processor, add pine nuts, Parmesan, and 3 Tbsp olive oil, and purée until smooth. Add parsley and process until parsley is finely chopped. Use at once, or cover with plastic wrap, pressing it onto surface, and refrigerate for up to 1 week.

eggplant, piquillo, and walnut pesto

eggplant 1 large, sliced
¼ inch thick

**sea salt and ground
pepper**

extra-virgin olive oil
2 Tbsp plus ½ cup

jarred piquillo peppers
½ cup drained

fresh mint 1 cup leaves

fresh flat-leaf parsley
½ cup leaves

**walnut halves or
pistachio nuts** ½ cup,
toasted

Manchego cheese
½ cup coarsely grated

garlic 1 clove, minced

serves 4–6
(with 1 lb pasta)

Preheat a grill or stove-top grill pan to high.

Season eggplant slices well on both sides with salt and pepper and lightly brush with 2 Tbsp olive oil. Place on grill rack or pan and grill, turning occasionally, until well charred on both sides, about 3 minutes. When cool to touch, transfer to a work surface and chop coarsely. Coarsely chop peppers. In a food processor, combine eggplant, peppers, ½ cup olive oil, mint, parsley, walnuts, cheese, and garlic. Pulse until ingredients are combined but mixture is still coarse. Use at once, or cover with plastic wrap, pressing it onto surface, and refrigerate for up to 1 week.

almond and mint pesto

almonds ¼ cup plus
2 Tbsp, unsalted, toasted,
and roughly chopped

extra-virgin olive oil
⅓ cup

garlic cloves 3, chopped

fresh mint 1 cup leaves

fresh basil ¾ cup leaves

Parmesan cheese
¼ cup freshly grated

**sea salt and ground
pepper**

serves 4–6
(with 1 lb pasta)

In a food processor, combine ¼ cup almonds, olive oil, and garlic and purée until smooth. Add mint, basil, and Parmesan and purée again until smooth. Season to taste with salt and pepper. Use at once, or cover with plastic wrap, pressing it onto surface, and refrigerate for up to 1 week.

When ready to serve, toss pesto with pasta, then garnish with 2 Tbsp almonds.

Chicken tastes best when it's roasted whole, and this classic dish makes a lot of people very happy. If you have friends coming over and are wondering what to cook, roast a chicken—and dress it up with a hit of flavor by tucking herbs or citrus under the skin before roasting.

roasted chicken with spring herbs

free-range organic chickens 2 whole, about 3½ lb each

fresh thyme, tarragon, and flat-leaf parsley 10 sprigs each, plus 2 sprigs each for garnish

extra-virgin olive oil 2 Tbsp

sea salt and ground pepper

serves 8

Preheat oven to 400°F. Pat chickens thoroughly dry with paper towels.

Place 1 chicken, breast side up, on a work surface. Starting at neck cavity, slip your fingers under skin and gently separate skin from breast meat on both sides, being careful not to tear skin. Push 4 of each type of herb sprig under skin, distributing them as evenly as you can. Repeat with second chicken and same number of sprigs. Place 1 of each type of herb sprig in cavity of each chicken.

Rub chickens all over with olive oil and season well inside and out with salt and pepper. Place chickens, breast side up, on a V-shaped roasting rack and place rack in a roasting pan. Roast until juices run clear when you pierce thickest part of thigh, about 1 hour.

Remove chickens from oven and allow to rest for 10 minutes. Using poultry shears, remove entire legs, then separate drumsticks from the thighs. Cut through center of each chicken, beginning at the wishbone, and then below breasts to separate breasts from carcass. Cut each breast in half through bones.

Arrange chicken pieces on a serving platter. Pour remaining juices on top of chicken (first skimming off excess fat with a spoon), or reserve for making a pan sauce (page 146). Garnish with reserved herb sprigs and serve at once.

CHANGE UP THE FLAVOR

Preserved lemon Replace herbs with 1 preserved lemon, cut into ⅛-inch slices, tucked between chicken skin and breast meat. Stir 2 Tbsp *ras el hanout* into olive oil before rubbing onto chickens.

Chorizo Remove casing from ½ lb raw chorizo, and divide into 4 balls. Tuck chorizo between chicken skin and breast meat, using your fingers to spread it over each breast.

Ricotta and herbs Mix together 2 cups ricotta cheese and 1 Tbsp chopped parsley, chives, or tarragon. Divide mixture into 4 balls. Push ricotta balls between chicken skin and breast meat, using your fingers to spread it over each breast.

pan sauce four ways

red currant and red wine sauce

dry red wine 2 cups

chicken stock 4 cups

red currant jelly 2 Tbsp

fresh red currants 1 cup

unsalted butter 2 Tbsp

sea salt and ground pepper

serves 8
(with roasted chicken from page 145)

After roasting chicken, transfer it to a platter. Using a spoon, skim off excess fat from pan juices. Place roasting pan over medium heat on 1 or 2 burners. To deglaze, add wine, bring to a boil, and boil for 2 minutes, stirring with a wooden spoon to scrape up any browned bits clinging to pan bottom. Add chicken stock, return to a boil, and cook until liquid has reduced by almost half. Stir in jelly and currants and simmer for 1 minute. Whisk in butter until fully incorporated. Season to taste with salt and pepper. Remove from heat and serve with the roasted chicken.

shallot, mustard, and thyme sauce

shallots ½ cup minced

dry white wine 2 cups

chicken stock 4 cups

unsalted butter 1 Tbsp

whole-grain mustard 1 Tbsp

fresh thyme 1 Tbsp minced

sea salt and ground pepper

serves 8
(with roasted chicken from page 145)

After roasting chicken, transfer it to a platter. Using a spoon, skim off excess fat from pan juices. Place roasting pan over medium heat on 1 or 2 burners. To deglaze, add shallots and wine, bring to a boil, and boil for 2 minutes, stirring with a wooden spoon to scrape up any browned bits clinging to pan bottom. Add chicken stock, return to a boil, and cook until liquid has reduced by half. Reduce to a simmer. Whisk in butter, mustard, and thyme until fully incorporated. Season to taste with salt and pepper. Remove from heat and serve with the roasted chicken.

white wine and tarragon sauce

dry white wine 2 cups

chicken stock 4 cups

unsalted butter 1 Tbsp

tarragon or Dijon mustard 1 Tbsp

fresh tarragon 1 Tbsp minced

fresh chives 1 Tbsp snipped

sea salt and ground pepper

serves 8
(with roasted chicken from page 145)

After roasting chicken, transfer it to a platter. Using a spoon, skim off excess fat from pan juices. Place roasting pan over medium heat on 1 or 2 burners. To deglaze, add wine, bring to a boil, and boil for 2 minutes, stirring with a wooden spoon to scrape up any browned bits clinging to pan bottom. Add chicken stock, return to a boil, and cook until liquid has reduced by half. Reduce to a simmer and whisk in butter and mustard until fully incorporated. Remove pan from heat and stir in tarragon and chives. Season to taste with salt and pepper. Serve with the roasted chicken.

port, fig, and orange sauce

tawny port 2 cups

chicken stock 4 cups

Black Mission figs 3, finely chopped

orange zest ¼ tsp grated

unsalted butter 2 Tbsp

fresh flat-leaf parsley 1 Tbsp minced

sea salt and ground pepper

serves 8
(with roasted chicken from page 145)

After roasting chicken, transfer it to a platter. Using a spoon, skim off excess fat from pan juices. Place roasting pan over medium heat on 1 or 2 burners. To deglaze, add port, bring to a boil, and boil for 2 minutes, stirring with a wooden spoon to scrape up any browned bits clinging to pan bottom. Add chicken stock, return to a boil, and cook until liquid has reduced by almost half. Stir in figs and orange zest and simmer for 1 minute. Whisk in butter until fully incorporated. Remove pan from heat and stir in parsley. Season to taste with salt and pepper. Serve with the roasted chicken.

grilled kebabs four ways

chicken with apricots and almonds

plain Greek yogurt
½ cup

coriander seeds 1 Tbsp,
crushed

garlic 1 clove, minced

ground turmeric, cumin,
and cayenne ½ tsp each

salt and ground pepper

boneless, skinless
chicken breasts 2

apricots 4

extra-virgin olive oil
4 Tbsp

blanched almonds
¼ cup, toasted

fresh mint 1¼ cups

lemon slices for serving

serves 4

In a bowl, stir together yogurt, coriander, garlic, turmeric, cumin, cayenne, and salt and pepper to taste. Cut chicken into 1-inch cubes, and toss well with yogurt mixture. Refrigerate for at least 6 hours or up to overnight.

Soak 8 bamboo skewers in water. Preheat a grill or stove-top grill pan to high and oil lightly. Cut each apricot into 6 wedges, then toss with 2 Tbsp olive oil. Thread about 4 chicken cubes and 3 apricot wedges onto each skewer, alternating them. Place skewers on hot grill and cook, turning once, until nicely charred, 4–5 minutes per side. Transfer to a platter, scatter with almonds and mint, and arrange lemon slices alongside. Drizzle with remaining olive oil and serve.

lamb with pomegranate

coarsely ground lamb
1 lb

garlic 2 cloves, minced

extra-virgin olive oil
1 Tbsp, plus more for
drizzling

ground cumin 1 tsp

ground cinnamon ¼ tsp

fresh flat-leaf parsley
½ cup chopped

salt and ground pepper

pomegranate 1

red onion ½, thinly sliced

wild arugula leaves
2 cups

lemon 1

serves 4

In a bowl, combine lamb, garlic, 1 Tbsp olive oil, cumin, cinnamon, and parsley. Season well with salt and pepper and mix well with your hands. Refrigerate for 3 hours.

Seed pomegranate (page 250), pat seeds dry, and set aside.

Soak 8 bamboo skewers in water. Preheat a grill or stove-top grill pan to medium-high and oil lightly. Divide lamb mixture into 8 portions. Using your hands, press each lamb portion onto a skewer, forming a long, thin patty.

Grill, turning once, until evenly charred, about 4 minutes per side. Transfer skewers to a platter, scatter with pomegranate seeds, red onion, and arugula, and drizzle with olive oil. Serve with lemon, cut into wedges.

chicken with olives and feta

boneless, skinless
chicken breasts 2, cut
into 1-inch cubes

garlic 1½ tsp minced

fresh thyme 1½ tsp
minced

fresh rosemary 1½ tsp
minced

extra-virgin olive oil
¼ cup

salt and ground pepper

feta cheese 1 cup
crumbled

pitted black olives such
as Kalamata ½ cup

fresh flat-leaf parsley
½ cup chopped

lemon 1

serves 4

In a small bowl, combine chicken, garlic, thyme, rosemary, and olive oil. Refrigerate for at least 6 hours or up to overnight.

Soak 8 bamboo skewers in water. Preheat a grill or stove-top grill pan to medium-high and oil lightly. Brush most of marinade from chicken pieces and thread about 5 pieces of chicken onto each skewer. Season well with salt and pepper. Grill, turning once, until nicely charred, 4–5 minutes per side. Transfer skewers to a platter and scatter feta, olives, and parsley on top. Serve with lemon, cut into wedges.

eggplant, zucchini, and squash

slender eggplants 2,
cut into ½-inch rounds

summer squash 2,
cut into ½-inch rounds

zucchini 2, cut into
½-inch rounds

fresh flat-leaf parsley
½ cup coarsely chopped

fresh mint ½ cup
coarsely chopped

grated lemon zest and
juice from 1 lemon

capers 1 Tbsp

extra-virgin olive oil
½ cup, plus more for
brushing

salt and ground pepper

serves 4

Soak 8 bamboo skewers in water. Preheat a grill or stove-top grill pan to medium-high and oil lightly. Using a sharp knife, score both cut sides of eggplant, squash, and zucchini rounds. Thread eggplant, squash, and zucchini onto skewers, using about 5 pieces per skewer and alternating them.

In a small bowl, stir together parsley, mint, lemon zest and juice, capers, and ½ cup olive oil. Season with salt and pepper and set aside.

Brush skewers with olive oil and place on hot grill. Grill, turning once, until nicely charred, 2–3 minutes per side. Transfer to a platter, drizzle herb sauce on top, and serve.

Pork is the most widely eaten meat in the world. This is borne out at our house. Try to source your meat from a good local supplier—it should be humanely raised on natural feeds. Or, order from Niman Ranch, which ships quality pork products.

pork chops with cranberry beans and thyme

CHANGE IT UP

We cook with lots of different fresh shell beans, many of which are in the market in late summer and early fall. Almost any variety will work here, from flageolet or Jacob's cattle to lima. Or, try borlotti or cannellini, and use sage in place of the thyme.

Working with 1 pork chop at a time, wrap a pancetta slice around the outer edge of each pork chop. Secure with a toothpick, season the chop with salt and pepper, and set aside. Repeat with remaining pork chops and pancetta.

In a saucepan over medium heat, warm 2 Tbsp olive oil. Add garlic and shallot and sauté until lightly golden, about 2 minutes. Add stock and bring to a boil. Add cranberry beans and thyme and simmer until beans burst, about 10 minutes. Stir in tomato paste and mustard and season well with salt and pepper. Turn off heat, but leave saucepan on burner to keep warm.

In a large sauté pan over medium-high heat, warm 2 Tbsp olive oil until shimmering. Sauté pork chops, turning once, until they are golden brown on both sides and pancetta is crispy, 4–6 minutes per side. If chops are browning too fast, reduce heat to medium.

Divide warm beans among individual plates, top each plate with a pork chop, and sprinkle with parsley. Drizzle with a little olive oil and serve at once.

pork chops 4, each 8 oz and 1 inch thick

pancetta or bacon 4 slices

sea salt and ground pepper

extra-virgin olive oil 4 Tbsp, plus more for drizzling

garlic 4 cloves, crushed

shallot 1, minced

chicken stock 3 cups

shelled fresh cranberry beans 2 cups

fresh thyme 1 Tbsp minced

tomato paste 2 Tbsp

whole-grain mustard 2 Tbsp

fresh flat-leaf parsley ½ cup coarsely chopped

serves 4

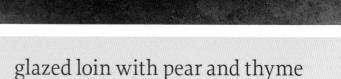

roasted loin with lentil salad

Puy lentils 1 cup

garlic 4 cloves, thinly sliced

bay leaf 1

chicken stock 6 cups

salt and ground pepper

pork tenderloin 1, about 1 lb, trimmed of excess fat

extra-virgin olive oil 1 Tbsp plus ¼ cup

fresh rosemary 4 sprigs

whole-grain mustard and red wine vinegar 1 Tbsp each

red onion ½, thinly sliced

fresh flat-leaf parsley ½ cup leaves

serves 4

In a saucepan, combine lentils, half of garlic, bay leaf, and stock. Season well. Bring to a boil, reduce heat, and simmer lentils until tender, about 45 minutes. Let cool in stock.

Preheat oven to 400°F. Season pork well. In an ovenproof sauté pan over medium-high heat, warm 1 Tbsp olive oil. Sear pork, turning occasionally, until well browned, 6–8 minutes total. Add remaining garlic and rosemary. Place in oven and roast until juices run clear when pork is pierced with a knife, 15–20 minutes. Remove from oven and let rest for 5 minutes.

Meanwhile, drain lentils and put in a bowl. Add ¼ cup olive oil, mustard, vinegar, onion, and parsley. Season and toss to combine. Spread on a serving platter. Slice pork thinly, arrange on lentils, and serve.

glazed loin with pear and thyme

pork tenderloin 1, about 1 lb, trimmed of excess fat

salt and ground pepper

extra-virgin olive oil 1 Tbsp

red onion 1, cut into ⅛-inch wedges

Forelle or Bosc pears 4, cored and each cut into 8 wedges

honey 2 Tbsp

balsamic vinegar 1 Tbsp

fresh thyme leaves from 12 sprigs

serves 4

Preheat oven to 400°F. Season pork well with salt and pepper.

In an ovenproof sauté pan over medium-high heat, warm olive oil until shimmering. Sear pork, turning occasionally, until well browned, 6–8 minutes total. Transfer pork to a plate. Add onion and pears to pan and sauté for 1 minute. Return pork to pan and drizzle with honey and vinegar. Scatter thyme leaves in pan. Place in oven and roast until juices run clear when pork is pierced with a knife, 15–20 minutes.

Remove pork from oven and let rest for 5 minutes. Cut into slices ½ inch thick. Divide pork and pears among 4 serving plates, drizzle with glaze from sauté pan, and serve.

roasted loin with pappardelle

pork tenderloin 1, about 1 lb, trimmed of excess fat

salt and ground pepper

olive oil 1 Tbsp

shiitake mushrooms 1 lb, stemmed and sliced

garlic 4 cloves, thinly sliced

fresh sage leaves ¼ cup small

chicken stock ½ cup

heavy cream ¼ cup

pappardelle pasta 1 lb, cooked al dente

Parmesan cheese ½ cup shredded

serves 4

Preheat oven to 400°F. Season pork with salt and pepper. In an ovenproof sauté pan over medium-high heat, warm olive oil. Sear pork, turning occasionally, until well browned, 6–8 minutes total. Transfer to a plate. Add mushrooms to pan and sauté until golden, about 3 minutes. Add garlic, cook for 1 minute, then add sage, stock, and cream and bring to a boil. Return pork to pan and place in oven. Roast, turning once and basting occasionally, until juices run clear when pierced, 15–20 minutes. While pork roasts, cook pasta.

Let pork rest for 5 minutes, then cut into very thin slices. Toss pasta with mushroom mixture in pan, then transfer to a platter. Arrange pork on top, sprinkle with Parmesan, salt, and pepper, and serve.

pork involtini with spinach

pork tenderloin 1, about 1 lb, butterflied and pounded to ¼-inch thickness

salt and ground pepper

prosciutto 6 slices

Fontina cheese ½ cup coarsely shredded

fresh sage 8 leaves

extra-virgin olive oil 2 Tbsp

garlic 4 cloves, thinly sliced

baby spinach leaves 1 lb

lemon 1, cut into wedges (optional)

serves 4

Preheat oven to 400°F. Lay pork loin flat and season well. Arrange prosciutto slices on top of pork, then scatter with cheese and sage. Starting at long side, roll loin up tightly, and secure with toothpicks at 1-inch intervals.

In an ovenproof sauté pan over medium-high heat, warm 1 Tbsp olive oil. Sear pork, turning occasionally, until well browned, 6–8 minutes total. Scatter half of garlic over pork, place in oven, and roast until juices run clear when pork is pierced, 10–15 minutes. Remove from oven and let rest for 5 minutes.

Heat 1 Tbsp oil in a saucepan over medium heat, add remaining garlic, and sauté for 1 minute. Add spinach, season, cover, and cook for 2 minutes. Slice pork and serve over spinach with lemon wedges (if using).

beef burgers with three toppings

classic beef burgers

ground beef chuck ¾ lb

ground beef sirloin ¾ lb

sea salt and ground pepper

toppings of choice (right and below)

serves 4

Lightly mix together by hand beef chuck and sirloin, 1 tsp salt, and ½ tsp pepper just until combined. Do not overmix. Divide beef into 4 equal portions, and form each into a patty about ¾ inch thick.

Preheat a grill to medium and oil grill rack. Grill burgers, turning once, for about 6 minutes for medium-rare, or about 10 minutes total for medium.

herbed mayonnaise and tomatoes

mayonnaise ½ cup

fresh lemon juice ½ tsp

fresh thyme ¼ tsp finely chopped

fresh chives ¼ tsp snipped

fresh basil ¼ tsp finely chopped

sea salt and ground pepper

brioche buns 4, split

heirloom tomatoes 2, sliced ¼ inch thick

avocados 2, sliced

Boston lettuce leaves 4

red onion slices 4 thin (optional)

serves 4

In a small bowl, stir together mayonnaise, lemon juice, thyme, chives, and basil. Season to taste with salt and pepper.

Prepare and cook burgers as directed (left). Transfer burgers to a cooler part of the grill while you grill buns, cut side down, until toasted, about 1 minute.

Spread cut sides of buns with herbed mayonnaise. Place burgers on bun bottoms and top with tomato, avocado, lettuce, and red onion (if using).

grilled onions and gorgonzola

focaccia bread slab about 6 inches square

Maui onions 2, sliced ½ inch thick

olive oil ¼ cup

sea salt and ground pepper

Gorgonzola cheese ½ lb

serves 4

Cut focaccia slab into 3-inch squares, and split squares horizontally. Set aside.

Prepare and cook burgers as directed (above).

Brush onion slices on both sides with olive oil and season well with salt and pepper. Alongside burgers, but on a hotter part of grill, grill onions, turning once, until nicely charred, 2–4 minutes per side. Crumble cheese on burgers during last 1–2 minutes of cooking. Serve burgers on focaccia, topped with onions.

chipotle barbecue sauce and bacon

Chipotle Barbecue Sauce (page 248) ½ cup, or purchased barbecue sauce

Vermont Cheddar cheese 4 slices

Kaiser rolls 4, split

bacon 8 slices, cooked

serves 4

Prepare and cook burgers as directed (above left). Place Cheddar slices on burgers during last 1–2 minutes of cooking.

While burgers are cooking, in a small saucepan over medium-low heat, warm barbecue sauce.

Spread cut sides of rolls with barbecue sauce. Place burgers on bun bottoms and top with 2 bacon slices.

T-bone steak on the grill, perhaps Tuscany's greatest contribution to world cuisine, calls for only a few ingredients, so all of them must be top quality. If you like, toss some rosemary sprigs on the coals to flavor the smoke.

grilled steak

. . . .

SERVE IT WITH

Tomato jam Serve sliced steak on a platter alongside a savory jam or relish, such as Tomato Jam (page 248).

Tarragon mustard With fresh herbs and jarred mustard, you can make a perfect sauce to accompany any steak (page 248). You can also mix fresh herbs (such as parsley or lemon verbena) and shallots into softened butter.

White beans and salsa verde Top each steak with a spoonful of Salsa Verde (page 249) or a pesto (page 143) and serve with a side of Slow-Cooked Tuscan White Beans (page 182).

Onion and corn salsa Top a T-bone with Red Onion and Corn Salsa (page 249); we like to grill the corn for a smoky taste.

To make a marinade, combine garlic, rosemary, 2 Tbsp olive oil, and 1½ tsp each salt and pepper and mix well. Divide marinade evenly between 2 large resealable plastic bags, and place 1 steak in each bag. Seal bags and massage marinade over meat. Place in refrigerator for at least 4 hours or up to overnight.

Remove steaks from bags and discard marinade. Scrape marinade off meat and allow meat to come to room temperature. Preheat a grill to medium-high.

Brush steaks lightly on both sides with olive oil and place on grill. Char well on both sides, turning occasionally, until an instant-read thermometer inserted into thickest part of meat away from bone registers 130°F to 140°F for medium-rare, 10–14 minutes total.

Transfer steaks to a cutting board and let rest for 5 minutes. Slice meat into ½-inch-thick slices and arrange on a platter. Serve with accompaniment of choice (left).

If Using 1-Inch-Thick T-bones or New York Strip Steaks
Grill as directed, reducing total cooking time to 4–6 minutes total for medium-rare. Transfer to a plate and let rest for 3 minutes before serving.

garlic 8 cloves, minced

fresh rosemary 4 sprigs, roughly chopped

extra-virgin olive oil 2 Tbsp, plus more for brushing

sea salt and ground pepper

steaks 2 T-bone, each 2 inches thick (about 2 lb total weight), or 2 sirloin, each 2 inches thick (about 1½ lb total weight)

CUT VARIATIONS

T-bone steaks 4, each 12–14 oz and 1 inch thick

New York strip steaks 4, each 10–12 oz and 1 inch thick

serves 4–6

We first made this pie with leftover short ribs (an unusual occurrence in our house!), and it soon became a favorite. It's ideal for preparing in advance: fill the gratin dishes with the ribs a day ahead, then top with freshly made mashed potatoes just before baking.

short rib shepherd's pie

SERVE IT WITH

A simple green salad is all you need to serve alongside this flavorful and filling dish. For dessert, we keep it light with a granita or sorbet.

DRESS IT UP

Shepherd's pie is made more special when cooked in individual gratin dishes.

Season ribs with salt and pepper and refrigerate for at least 6 hours or up to overnight. Bring to room temperature and season again with salt and pepper.

Preheat oven to 350°F. Heat a large sauté pan over high heat until hot. Add olive oil and heat until shimmering. In batches, sear ribs on all sides, turning as needed, until well browned. Transfer to a Dutch oven. Pour off all but 2 Tbsp fat from sauté pan and return to medium heat. Add onion, celery, garlic, and carrot and sauté until beginning to caramelize, about 5 minutes. Add wine, bay leaves, and thyme, raise heat to medium-high, and boil to reduce wine by half. Add stock, bring to a boil, and pour contents of pan over ribs. They should be just covered with liquid; add stock as needed.

Cover tightly and braise in oven, adding stock as needed to maintain liquid level, until a fork slides easily through meat, about 2½ hours. Skim off any fat from surface, let ribs cool in liquid until they can be handled, then remove ribs from pot and pull meat from bones. Shred meat into bite-sized pieces, return to Dutch oven, and discard bones.

While ribs are cooling, in a saucepan, cook potatoes in boiling salted water until tender, about 15 minutes. Drain, dry in pan over low heat, then pass through ricer back into warm pan. In a small saucepan, heat milk and butter until mixture is steaming. Pour into potatoes, add egg yolk, and fold to mix well.

Raise oven temperature to 400°F. Transfer contents of Dutch oven to a 9-by-13-inch baking dish or divide among individual gratin dishes. Cover top(s) evenly with potatoes. Bake until topping is golden, 35–40 minutes. Serve at once.

beef short ribs 4, each 2¼–2½ lb

sea salt and ground pepper

extra-virgin olive oil 2 Tbsp

onion 1 large, chopped

celery 2 stalks, chopped

garlic 6 cloves, crushed

carrot 1, chopped

dry red wine such as Syrah 3½ cups

bay leaves 3

fresh thyme 1 Tbsp leaves

beef stock 4 cups, or as needed

Yukon gold potatoes 1½ lb, peeled and quartered

milk ¼ cup

unsalted butter 4 Tbsp

egg yolk 1, beaten

serves 6–8

pot roast three ways

classic pot roast

chuck roast 4 lb, tied

salt and ground pepper

flour ¼ cup

olive oil 6 Tbsp

onion 1, cut into 8 pieces

garlic 6 cloves, crushed

beef stock 5 cups

bay leaves 2

fresh thyme, rosemary, and parsley 2 sprigs each

button mushrooms 1 lb, halved

carrots 1 lb, cut into 1-inch pieces

small potatoes 1½ lb, halved

cornstarch 1½ tsp

serves 8

Preheat oven to 300°F. Place roast in a large bowl, season well with salt and pepper, and dust with flour. Heat a Dutch oven over medium heat, add 2 Tbsp olive oil, and heat until shimmering. Add roast and sear until browned all over. Transfer to a plate. Add onion and garlic to Dutch oven and sauté, stirring occasionally, until softened, about 5 minutes. Add stock, bay leaves, and herb sprigs and bring to a boil. Return roast to Dutch oven, cover, and place in oven. Braise for 2½ hours, turning meat after 1¼ hours.

Meanwhile, in a frying pan, heat 4 Tbsp olive oil over medium-high heat until shimmering. Add mushrooms, season well with salt and pepper, and sauté until golden brown, about 5 minutes. Set aside.

After roast has cooked for 2½ hours, carefully transfer it to a plate. Leave oven on. Using a fine-mesh sieve lined with a cheesecloth, strain cooking liquid into a bowl. Discard solids and, using a spoon, skim off fat from surface of liquid. Return meat to Dutch oven and add sautéed mushrooms, carrots, potatoes, and strained cooking liquid. Mix cornstarch with 2 Tbsp water and add to Dutch oven. Place on stove top over high heat, bring to a boil, then return to oven to continue braising until vegetables are tender, about 30 minutes more.

Transfer roast to a cutting board and remove strings. Cut into thick slices and arrange on a platter along with roasted vegetables. Spoon cooking liquid on top, and serve at once.

japanese pot roast

fresh ginger 4 slices

mirin 1 cup

reduced-sodium soy sauce 1 cup

star anise pods 2

shiitake mushrooms 1 lb, stemmed and halved

daikon 1 lb, peeled and cut into 1-inch pieces

green onions 1 cup thinly sliced

cilantro ½ cup chopped

hot English mustard (optional)

serves 8

Prepare pot roast (above) as directed, adding ginger with onion and garlic. Replace 2 cups beef stock with mirin and soy sauce. Replace sprigs of thyme, parsley, and rosemary and bay leaves with star anise. Replace button mushrooms with shiitake mushrooms and replace carrots with daikon. To serve, garnish with green onions and cilantro. Serve with hot English mustard (if using).

ancho pot roast

tomatillos 6, husked

chipotle chiles in adobo 4, chopped

canned hominy 6 cups, drained

sour cream 1 cup

green onions 1 cup thinly sliced

avocados 2, diced

cilantro 2 Tbsp, torn

serves 8

Prepare pot roast (above) as directed through adding onion and garlic. Omit the herb sprigs, mushrooms, carrots, potatoes, and cornstarch. Add the stock, bay leaves, tomatillos, and chipotle chiles to onion and garlic and bring to a boil. Return roast to Dutch oven, cover, and place in oven. Braise for 2½ hours, turning meat after 1¼ hours. During last 30 minutes of braising, add hominy. Serve sour cream, green onions, avocados, and cilantro on the side for guests to add as desired.

While the Chinese are the biggest connoisseurs of duck, this classic combination of duck and figs is more French in style. Vinegar usually works well with fruits and here you could easily substitute firm plums or peaches if figs are not your thing or in season.

duck breasts with roasted figs and balsamic glaze

DRESS IT UP

Thanks to the shapely figs, this is a dramatic-looking dish. Slice the duck and place it on a platter; top with the figs and balsamic glaze. Alternatively, divide among individual plates: place 2 or 3 slices of duck on each plate, top with a fig, and drizzle with glaze.

PAIR IT WITH

Serve this dish with a big, fruity red—maybe a California Petite Sirah or an Italian Primitivo.

Preheat oven to 400°F. Using a sharp knife, trim away any visible fat from each duck breast to create an even ¼-inch-thick layer. Then score skin side of each breast, cutting through skin but not into flesh and creating a ¼-inch crosshatch. Season breasts well with salt and pepper on both sides. Set aside.

Using a paring knife, cut a small cross in the tops of figs. Spread figs open, season with salt and pepper, and place on a rimmed baking sheet. Pour vinegar over figs and scatter with thyme sprigs. Roast, basting figs with vinegar every 4–5 minutes, until nicely glazed, 12–15 minutes. Keep figs warm in oven.

Heat a large, dry frying pan over medium-high heat. When pan is hot, add duck breasts, skin side down, and sear until skin is crisp and golden brown, 6–7 minutes. Turn and cook until lightly brown on other side, 3–4 minutes longer for medium rare. Transfer to a platter and let rest for 3–4 minutes.

Thinly slice duck breasts on the diagonal. Arrange slices on a serving platter with figs, drizzle with balsamic glaze from baking sheet, and serve at once.

skin-on, boneless duck breasts 6, 2¼ lb total weight

sea salt and ground pepper

Black Mission figs 8 ripe

aged balsamic vinegar ½ cup

fresh thyme 8 sprigs

serves 4–6

We love summer lamb. Lamb is traditionally associated with spring, of course, but after a few more months of grazing, lambs yield meat with a richer taste that marries well with bold flavors like garlic, feta, or rosemary.

roasted lamb chops with garlic and rosemary

racks of lamb 2, each 7 or 8 ribs and 1½–2 lb, frenched by butcher

garlic 4 cloves, thinly sliced

fresh rosemary 4 sprigs, roughly chopped

extra-virgin olive oil 2½ Tbsp

sea salt and ground pepper

serves 4

Place lamb racks in a large bowl. Add garlic, rosemary, and 2 Tbsp olive oil, and turn racks to coat evenly with ingredients. Transfer racks with seasonings to a large resealable plastic bag and refrigerate for at least 6 hours or up to overnight.

Preheat oven to 425°F. Scrape off most of marinade from lamb and reserve. Season lamb with salt and pepper and allow to come to room temperature. Heat a large frying pan over high heat, add remaining 1½ tsp olive oil, and heat until shimmering. Place lamb racks in pan and sear on all sides until well browned.

Transfer lamb racks to a rimmed baking sheet and scatter reserved marinade on top. Roast until an instant-read thermometer inserted into thickest part of meat away from bone registers 130°F to 140°F for medium-rare, about 15 minutes.

Remove lamb from oven and let rest for 5–10 minutes. To serve, slice lamb into individual chops.

SERVE IT WITH

Summer vegetables As the lamb roasts, you can grill up a spread of summer vegetables (page 53). Or, drizzle vegetables with olive oil, sprinkle with sea salt and pepper, and roast alongside the lamb. Tomatoes are a good choice for roasting; toss some unpeeled garlic cloves into the roasting pan as well.

Greek salad Lamb is the most popular meat in Greece, so it's no shocker that a classic Greek side salad (page 249) makes an excellent accompaniment.

Gremolata We enjoy the bright herb and citrus flavors of Gremolata (page 248) with many meat and fish dishes, especially this one. It is traditionally served with osso buco (braised veal shank).

sides

When we cook, we focus on simplicity and try not to be too fussy. Sometimes we'll just add a little olive oil and salt, or a spritz of lemon juice, and that's it. Keep your food fresh and simple.

Butternut squash tastes sweet and nutty, quite similar to sweet potato. High in vitamins A and C, it's an excellent source of nutrients. This dish is one of Alison's favorites and is equally good the day after for leftovers.

warm squash salad with mint

. . . .

SERVE IT WITH

This salad makes a wonderful side dish for roasted meats or poultry. It will add a breath of fresh air to your next Thanksgiving dinner! A Pinot Noir would complement the smooth, rich flavor of the squash.

MAKE IT A MEAL

To bulk up this salad, chop the squash into cubes instead of rings before roasting. Roughly chop the onion instead of slicing it. Just before serving, toss the salad with 4 cups cooked couscous or quinoa (page 192).

Preheat oven to 400°F. Peel squash then cut crosswise into slices 1 inch thick and, using a spoon, scrape out seeds and discard.

Lightly oil 2 rimmed baking sheets. Arrange squash in a single layer on sheets and brush on both sides with ¼ cup olive oil. Sprinkle with salt and pepper. Roast, turning once, until just tender, about 30 minutes.

Meanwhile, make a dressing. In a small bowl, whisk together ¼ cup olive oil, vinegar, onion, oregano, garlic, and red pepper flakes. Season to taste with salt and pepper.

Transfer squash to a platter. Pour dressing over top and let stand until flavors have blended, about 20 minutes. Garnish with mint and serve at once.

butternut squash 2 small, 2½ lb each

extra-virgin olive oil ½ cup

sea salt and ground pepper

red wine vinegar ¼ cup

red onion 1 small, very thinly sliced

fresh oregano 1 tsp minced

garlic 1 clove, thinly sliced

red pepper flakes ½ tsp

fresh mint ¼ cup leaves

serves 8

flash-fried bok choy

sesame oil 1 Tbsp

baby bok choy
10 heads, halved
lengthwise

chicken stock 1 cup

garlic 2 cloves, thinly
sliced

**reduced-sodium soy
sauce** 1 Tbsp

red pepper flakes
½ tsp

serves 6–8

Heat a wok or sauté pan over high heat.
Add sesame oil and heat until shimmering.
Add bok choy and cook, stirring and
tossing constantly, until starting to wilt on
ends, about 2 minutes. Add chicken stock,
garlic, and soy sauce. Bring to a simmer
and cook until greens are just tender when
pierced with a knife, 2–3 minutes. Stir in
red pepper flakes. Transfer to a platter
and serve at once.

tuscan kale with anchovy

Tuscan kale 4 bunches,
about 2 lb total weight

extra-virgin olive oil
2 Tbsp

garlic 2 cloves, minced

**olive-oil packed
anchovy fillets** 8,
drained and minced

sea salt

red pepper flakes ½ tsp

fresh lemon juice 1 Tbsp

lemon zest 2 tsp
shredded

serves 8

Trim away tough stem ends of kale.
Coarsely chop kale into bite-sized pieces.

In a large frying pan over medium-high
heat, warm olive oil until shimmering. Add
garlic and anchovies and cook, stirring, just
until garlic is golden, about 1 minute. Add
kale, ½ tsp salt, and 1 cup water. Cook,
stirring occasionally, until kale is tender
to the bite, about 10 minutes. Stir in red
pepper flakes and lemon juice and zest.
Transfer to a platter and serve at once.

broccoli rabe with pickled onion

....

red onion 1 small, thinly sliced

Champagne vinegar ¼ cup

sugar 1 tsp

broccoli rabe 2 bunches, about 4 lb total weight

extra-virgin olive oil 2 Tbsp

sea salt and ground pepper

serves 8

Put onion in a small heatproof bowl. In a small saucepan over medium heat, combine vinegar and sugar and bring to a boil. Remove vinegar mixture from heat, pour over onion, and marinate for 15 minutes (onion will wilt). Drain onion in a fine-mesh sieve and rinse briefly with cold running water. Set aside.

Trim away tough ends of broccoli rabe. Chop into 3-inch pieces.

Heat olive oil in a large frying pan over medium-high heat. Add broccoli rabe and 1 tsp salt and cook, stirring occasionally, until tender to the bite, about 5 minutes. Add onion, season to taste with pepper, and stir to combine. Transfer to a serving platter and serve at once.

sesame-ginger spinach

....

fresh ginger 1-inch piece, finely grated

fresh lemon juice from 1 lemon

toasted sesame oil 1 Tbsp

garlic ½ tsp grated

spinach 1 bunch, about 1 lb, stems intact

sea salt and ground pepper

serves 4–6

In a small bowl, whisk together ginger, lemon juice, sesame oil, and garlic to make a dressing.

Swish spinach bunch well in a large bowl of water to remove any sand or dirt. Bring a large pot of water to a boil and blanch the whole spinach bunch just until wilted, about 30 seconds. Remove spinach with a wire skimmer and pat dry with paper towels. Transfer to a platter and season to taste with salt and pepper. Pour dressing over spinach and serve at once.

In 1604, Caravaggio was rumored to have thrown a plate of fried artichokes in a waiter's face for not knowing whether they were prepared in oil or butter. Thankfully, nothing like this happens in our house. We love artichokes, whatever the cooking medium.

fried artichokes with aioli

egg yolks 3, at room temperature

garlic 2 cloves, minced

sea salt

extra-virgin olive oil 1 cup

fresh lemon juice 2 Tbsp

lemons 4

artichokes 4

grapeseed oil for deep-frying

flour 1 cup

serves 4

To make aioli, combine egg yolks, garlic, and 1 tsp salt in a food processor. Process until ingredients are combined, about 30 seconds. With motor running, very slowly dribble in olive oil to form a thick emulsion, drizzling faster as mixture thickens. Add lemon juice, process until well combined, and transfer aioli to a small bowl. Set aside.

Fill a bowl with cold water. Halve 2 lemons and squeeze juice into water. Working with 1 artichoke at a time, snap off tough outer leaves until you reach pale green inner leaves, then cut off thorny tips. Leave stems intact, but trim off base and then peel stems with a vegetable peeler, starting where leaves were snapped off to reveal tender flesh. Cut each artichoke in half lengthwise, then cut each half in half again lengthwise. Using a paring knife, cut away bristly choke from artichoke quarters. As each artichoke is trimmed, drop the quarters in lemon water.

Pour grapeseed oil into a large saucepan to a depth of 3 or 4 inches and heat to 325°F on a deep-frying thermometer. While oil heats, put flour in a large bowl. Remove artichokes from water and carefully dry with paper towels. Add artichokes to bowl of flour and toss to dust lightly, shaking off any excess. When oil is ready, working in batches, carefully add artichokes to pan. Fry until crisp and golden, 3–4 minutes. Using a slotted spoon, transfer to paper towels to drain, and season with salt. Let oil return to 325°F between batches. Serve at once with aioli and remaining lemons, cut into wedges.

CHANGE IT UP

You can vary the aioli to suit your taste. Stir in chopped fresh herbs such as dill or parsley, chopped capers, or even a pinch of cayenne pepper for a kick of spice.

PAIR IT WITH

Fried artichokes are a classic starter in Rome, but we enjoy serving these as a side dish with fish or pasta. Artichokes are famous for not pairing well with any wine. However, we've found that a light rosé or a Grüner Veltliner from Austria works quite nicely.

gratin four ways

leek gratin

leeks 8 young, white and pale green parts

ricotta cheese 1 cup

Gruyère cheese 1 cup shredded

whole-grain mustard 1 Tbsp

sea salt and ground pepper

panko 1 cup

fresh flat-leaf parsley ½ tsp chopped

fresh thyme ½ tsp chopped

serves 4

Preheat oven to 375°F. Butter 4 individual 4-by-6-inch gratin dishes.

Bring a large pot of salted water to a boil. Add leeks, reduce heat to a gentle simmer, and poach until just tender when pierced with a knife, about 8 minutes. Drain leeks, let cool until cool enough to handle, and cut into 1½-inch chunks. Set aside.

In a bowl, stir together ricotta, Gruyère, and mustard. Divide leeks among prepared gratin dishes and add a pinch of salt and pepper. Top with cheese mixture and sprinkle with panko, parsley, and thyme. Bake until golden brown, 15–20 minutes, then serve.

rainbow chard gratin

Rainbow Swiss chard 3 lb (about 2 bunches)

extra-virgin olive oil 1 Tbsp

onion 1, thinly sliced

garlic 1 clove, minced

fresh thyme 1½ tsp leaves

sea salt and ground pepper

ricotta cheese 2 cups

Gruyère cheese 1 cup shredded

Dijon mustard 1 Tbsp

fresh bread crumbs 1 cup

serves 4–6

Preheat oven to 375°F. Butter a 12-inch oval gratin dish. Cut chard leaves from stems. Keeping leaves and stems separate, cut both into 1-inch pieces. Heat oil in a large frying pan over medium heat until shimmering. Add stems and sauté for 2 minutes. Add onion, garlic, and thyme and cook until onion is softened, about 6 minutes. Add leaves and cook, stirring, until wilted, about 4 minutes. Season with salt and pepper. Transfer greens to a colander and drain well, pressing with the back of a spoon to remove excess liquid.

In a bowl, stir together cheeses and mustard. Add chard and stir to mix well. Spread chard mixture in prepared dish and scatter bread crumbs on top. Bake until topping is golden, about 20 minutes, then serve.

cauliflower gratin

unsalted butter 3 Tbsp

flour 4½ tsp

half-and-half 1 cup

prepared horseradish 3 Tbsp

white wine vinegar ½ tsp

freshly grated nutmeg, sea salt, and ground pepper

cauliflower florets 4 cups, steamed

Fontina cheese 1 cup shredded

Dijon mustard 1½ tsp

panko 1 cup

serves 4

Preheat oven to 375°F. Butter 4 individual 4-by-6-inch gratin dishes.

In a large, heavy saucepan over medium heat, melt 1½ Tbsp butter. Add flour and cook, stirring, for 2 minutes. Do not let it brown. Whisking constantly, gradually add half-and-half and stir until sauce boils and thickens, 4 minutes. Stir in 2 Tbsp horseradish and vinegar. Season to taste with nutmeg, salt, and pepper. Add cauliflower and toss to coat. Divide evenly among prepared dishes, and sprinkle with cheese.

In a heavy frying pan over medium heat, melt 1½ Tbsp butter. Stir in mustard and 1 Tbsp horseradish. Add panko and cook, stirring, until golden brown, 9 minutes. Sprinkle over gratins. Bake until heated through, about 15 minutes, then serve.

chicory and radicchio gratin

chicory 4 heads, halved lengthwise

Treviso radicchio 2 heads, quartered lengthwise

heavy cream 1 cup

fresh goat cheese ¼ lb

sea salt and ground pepper

pecorino cheese ½ cup freshly grated

panko 1 cup

serves 4

Preheat oven to 375°F. Butter 4 individual 4-by-6-inch gratin dishes.

Bring a large pot of salted water to a boil. Add chicory and blanch for 3 minutes. After 1 minute, add radicchio and blanch for 2 minutes. Remove chicory and radicchio with tongs, drain, and divide among prepared dishes. Pour cream over vegetables and dot with goat cheese. Season with salt and pepper. Sprinkle with pecorino cheese and panko. Bake until topping is golden brown, about 15 minutes, then serve.

tomato and white bean salad

....

**Slow-Roasted Tomatoes
(far right)** made with
assorted tomatoes

**Slow-Cooked
Tuscan White Beans**
(page 182)

fresh oregano ¼ cup
leaves

extra-virgin olive oil
¼ cup

Champagne vinegar
¼ cup

**sea salt and ground
pepper**

serves 4–6

Place roasted tomatoes in a bowl. Add
cooked white beans, oregano, olive oil, and
vinegar and toss to combine. Season to
taste with salt and pepper. Serve in bowl
or transfer to a platter.

tomato, melon, and pepita salad

....

extra-virgin olive oil
¼ cup

Champagne vinegar
2 Tbsp

**Green Zebra and/or
red heirloom tomatoes**
6–8, cut into 8 wedges
each

cantaloupe ½, peeled,
cut into ¾-inch wedges,
then roughly chopped

pepitas (pumpkin
seeds) ¼ cup toasted

fresh basil 10 leaves,
torn

fresh mint 10 leaves, torn

**sea salt and ground
pepper**

serves 4–6

In a large bowl, whisk together olive oil
and vinegar. Add tomatoes, cantaloupe,
pepitas, basil, and mint. Season to taste
with salt and pepper and toss to combine.
Transfer to a platter and serve.

panzanella toasts

. . . .

white artisanal bread
6 slices, ½ inch thick

garlic 1 clove, halved

**cherry or grape
tomatoes** 2 cups, halved

shallot 1, minced

fresh basil ¼ cup leaves,
torn

fresh oregano 1 tsp
leaves

**sea salt and ground
pepper**

serves 4–6

Toast or grill bread slices. Rub toasts
on one side with garlic.

In a bowl, toss tomatoes with shallot. Top
garlic-rubbed side of toasts with tomatoes
and sprinkle with basil and oregano.
Season to taste with salt and pepper
and serve.

slow-roasted tomatoes

. . . .

tomatoes 8–10 plum or
2 cups cherry tomatoes,
halved lengthwise

extra-virgin olive oil
about ¼ cup

sugar about 1 tsp

garlic 2 cloves, thinly
sliced

**sea salt and ground
pepper**

serves 4–6

Preheat oven to 300°F. Lightly oil a rimmed
baking sheet. Arrange tomatoes, cut side
up, on prepared baking sheet. Drizzle with
olive oil and sprinkle evenly with sugar,
garlic, and generous amounts of salt and
pepper. Roast tomatoes until deep red and
wrinkled, 2–2½ hours for medium or plum
tomatoes and 1 hour for cherry tomatoes.

Remove from oven and let cool on baking
sheet. Serve warm or at room temperature.

Until the sixteenth century, the Italians were the only Europeans who appreciated the cauliflower. This recipe, a Jamie specialty, gives a nod to the vegetable's Italian heritage and, along with the broccoli recipe, is a good match with most meats.

roasted cauliflower with pine nuts and raisins

cauliflower 2 heads (about 3 lb total weight)

extra-virgin olive oil 4 Tbsp

sea salt and ground pepper

red wine vinegar 2 Tbsp

fresh lemon juice 2 Tbsp

golden raisins 3 Tbsp, soaked in boiling water for 30 minutes and drained

fresh flat-leaf parsley 2 Tbsp coarsely chopped

lemon zest 1 tsp shredded

pine nuts 3 Tbsp, toasted

serves 8

Preheat oven to 425°F. Core cauliflower heads and cut into florets. Place on a rimmed baking sheet, drizzle with 2 Tbsp olive oil, and season with salt and pepper. Roast, turning once, until just tender, 25–30 minutes.

Meanwhile, make a vinaigrette. In a small bowl, whisk together 2 Tbsp olive oil, vinegar, and lemon juice. Season to taste with salt and pepper and stir in raisins.

Transfer warm cauliflower to a serving dish and drizzle with vinaigrette. Sprinkle with parsley, lemon zest, and pine nuts. To marry the flavors, let cool to room temperature before serving.

CHANGE IT UP

Capers or pitted and chopped green olives can be substituted here for the raisins. A sprinkle of red pepper flakes is a welcome addition for anyone who likes spicy food.

roasted broccoli with orange zest and almonds

broccoli 2 heads (about 3 lb total weight)

extra-virgin olive oil 4 Tbsp

sea salt and ground pepper

fresh orange juice 2 Tbsp

orange zest 2 tsp grated

almonds ¼ cup, toasted and coarsely chopped

serves 8

Preheat oven to 425°F. Trim broccoli heads and cut into florets. In a large bowl, toss broccoli with 3 Tbsp olive oil. Transfer to a rimmed baking sheet and season with salt and pepper. Roast until just tender and stalks begin to brown, about 25 minutes.

Transfer roasted broccoli to a serving dish, drizzle with 1 Tbsp olive oil and orange juice, sprinkle with orange zest and almonds, and serve.

SERVE IT UP

Often we'll place a platter of roasted vegetables in the middle of the table for all to share. Other times we'll plate individual servings alongside the main dish.

beans four ways

slow-cooked tuscan white beans

. . . .

dried white beans such as northern, navy, or cannellini 2 cups, soaked overnight in water to cover, drained, and rinsed

sea salt and ground pepper

fresh rosemary 2 sprigs

bay leaves 2

garlic 4 cloves, lightly crushed

extra-virgin olive oil ¼ cup

serves 6

In a large, heavy pot, combine beans, 1 Tbsp salt, rosemary, bay leaves, garlic, and 8 cups water. Cover and slowly bring to a simmer over low heat. Simmer, uncovered, until beans are tender but not mushy, about 45 minutes. Remove from heat and let cool, covered, for 15 minutes.

Drain beans. Discard rosemary, bay leaves, and garlic, if desired. Sprinkle with pepper, drizzle with olive oil, and serve.

summer bean and corn salad

. . . .

corn 2 ears, husks and silk removed

yellow wax beans ¾ lb, trimmed

green beans ¾ lb, trimmed

red onion 1 small, thinly sliced

extra-virgin olive oil ¼ cup

white wine vinegar 2 Tbsp

fresh tarragon 1 tsp minced

fresh chervil 8 sprigs

sea salt and ground pepper

serves 6

Bring a large pot three-fourths full of salted water to a boil. Cook corn until crisp-tender, about 5 minutes. Remove corn with tongs, reserving water, and set aside. Add wax beans to hot water, cook for 1 minute, then add green beans. Cook until beans are crisp-tender, about 2 minutes more. While beans cook, prepare a bowl of ice water. Drain beans and immediately transfer them to ice water to stop the cooking.

Cut kernels from corn cobs, letting kernels fall into a shallow bowl. Add beans and onion to bowl, drizzle with olive oil and vinegar, and toss to combine. Sprinkle with tarragon and chervil and season to taste with salt and pepper. Serve at room temperature, or cover, chill, and serve cold.

black bean and poblano salad

....

poblano chiles 2

extra-virgin olive oil
¼ cup

red wine vinegar 2 Tbsp

Dijon mustard 1 Tbsp

sugar 1 tsp

**ground cumin and
paprika** ½ tsp each

salt and ground pepper

black beans 2 cans
(15 oz each)

red onion ½

pear tomatoes 1 pint
mixed, halved

**queso fresco and
chopped cilantro**
for garnish

serves 6

Preheat oven to 400°F. Put poblanos on
a rimmed baking sheet and roast, turning
occasionally, until softened and blistered,
about 25 minutes. Remove from oven,
transfer to a bowl, cover, and let cool
in their own steam.

Meanwhile, whisk together olive oil,
vinegar, mustard, sugar, cumin, paprika,
and salt and pepper to taste. Set vinaigrette
aside. Rinse and drain beans, and finely
dice onion.

When poblanos are cool enough to
handle, remove skins, ribs, and seeds and
cut into ½-inch dice. In a bowl, combine
chiles, black beans, onion, tomatoes, and
vinaigrette. Toss to combine. Season to
taste with salt and pepper and sprinkle
queso fresco and cilantro on top. Serve.

romano beans with almonds

....

Italian (romano) beans
1 lb, trimmed and cut
on diagonal into 2-inch
pieces

extra-virgin olive oil
2 Tbsp

lemon ½

almonds ¼ cup, toasted
and roughly chopped

sea salt

serves 4

Bring a large pot three-fourths full of salted
water to a boil. Add beans and boil until
tender, about 3 minutes. Drain well and
place in a bowl.

Drizzle beans with olive oil. Squeeze juice
from lemon half over beans and stir in
almonds and salt to taste. Serve at once.

gnocchi with two toppings

gnocchi

baking potatoes
3 large (about 1½ lb total weight)

flour 2 cups, or as needed

sea salt

topping of choice (below)

serves 8–10
as side dish

serves 4–6
as main course

Preheat oven to 350°F. Prick each potato several times. Place potatoes on oven rack and bake until flesh is very tender when pierced with a knife, about 1 hour. Transfer to a rimmed baking sheet to cool.

When potatoes are cool enough to handle, cut in half lengthwise. With a large metal spoon, scoop out flesh and pass it through a potato ricer, letting it fall onto baking sheet. Using a spatula, spread out potato and let cool completely.

In a large mixing bowl, stir together 1½ cups flour and 1 tsp salt. Slowly blend flour mixture into potatoes, using your hands to form a rough and shaggy dough. The dough should pull away from your hands and feel like pizza dough. Add more flour if necessary to achieve the desired consistency, but do not overmix.

Sprinkle ¼ cup flour on a clean work surface. Dust a clean rimmed baking sheet with flour. Shape dough into a ball and divide into 4 equal portions. Using both hands, roll each portion into a log about ½ inch in diameter. Cut each log into 1-inch pieces. To form gnocchi, dip a fork into flour and gently press each piece of dough with the back of the tines. Place shaped gnocchi on prepared baking sheet.

Bring a large pot three-fourths full of water to a rolling boil and add 1 Tbsp salt. Drop about 8 gnocchi at a time into boiling water. Cook until gnocchi rise to the surface, about 3 minutes. Remove with a slotted spoon and transfer to a bowl. Cover to keep warm. Serve with topping of choice.

wild mushroom topping

extra-virgin olive oil
2 Tbsp

morel mushrooms
1 cup coarsely chopped

chanterelle mushrooms
1 cup coarsely chopped

garlic 2 cloves, thinly sliced

shallot 1, minced

sea salt and ground pepper

Parmesan cheese ¼ cup freshly grated

fresh flat-leaf parsley ¼ cup chopped

serves 8–10
as side dish

serves 4–6
as main course

Prepare and cook gnocchi as directed above.

In a large sauté pan over medium-high heat, warm olive oil. Add morels and chanterelles and sauté for 2 minutes. Add garlic and shallot and sauté for 1 minute more. Add cooked gnocchi to pan and gently stir to combine. Season well with salt and pepper. Transfer to a serving platter, sprinkle with Parmesan and parsley, and serve at once.

radicchio and gorgonzola topping

extra-virgin olive oil
2 Tbsp

radicchio 1 head, shredded

sea salt and ground pepper

Gorgonzola cheese ½ cup crumbled

pine nuts ½ cup, toasted

serves 8–10
as side dish

serves 4–6
as main course

Prepare and cook gnocchi as directed above.

In a large saucepan over high heat, warm olive oil. Add radicchio and sauté until it wilts, about 2 minutes. Season well with salt and pepper. Place cooked gnocchi on a platter, scatter Gorgonzola on top, and top with radicchio. Sprinkle with pine nuts and serve at once.

whole potatoes with spring herbs

small white creamers
or small new potatoes
1 lb

sea salt and ground
pepper

extra-virgin olive oil
1 Tbsp

mixed fresh spring
herbs such as chervil,
dill, and tarragon
1 Tbsp chopped

serves 4

In a large pot over high heat, combine
potatoes, 1 tsp salt, and water to cover by
2 inches and bring to a boil. Cover, reduce
heat, and simmer until potatoes are knife-
tender, 12–15 minutes.

Drain potatoes and transfer to a bowl.
Add olive oil, 1 tsp salt, and ½ tsp pepper
and toss gently. Sprinkle herbs on top and
serve at once.

roasted fingerlings with garlic

baby fingerling
potatoes 1 lb, halved
lengthwise

extra-virgin olive oil
¼ cup

fresh rosemary 4 sprigs,
minced

sea salt and ground
pepper

garlic 3 cloves, thinly
sliced

serves 4

Place potatoes in a bowl, and add olive
oil and rosemary. Season well with salt
and pepper.

Arrange potatoes in a single layer on a
rimmed baking sheet. Roast for 10 minutes,
stir, and roast for another 10 minutes.
Scatter garlic on top of potatoes and roast
until potatoes are golden brown and knife-
tender, about 10 minutes more. Transfer
to a platter, sprinkle with salt, and serve
at once.

red potatoes with gruyère

....

small red potatoes 1 lb
extra-virgin olive oil
2 Tbsp
sea salt
Gruyère cheese ¼ cup
shredded

serves 4

Preheat oven to 375°F. Prick each potato with a fork in 2 or 3 places. Place on a rimmed baking sheet and toss with olive oil and 1 tsp salt. Roast potatoes until knife-tender, about 50 minutes.

Using a sharp knife, split each potato open without cutting all the way through. Gently spread halves open and sprinkle a little Gruyère and salt in each potato. Serve warm, as cheese begins to melt.

new potatoes with crème fraîche

....

new potatoes 1 lb
sea salt and ground
pepper
crème fraîche ¼ cup
fresh chives 2 tsp
snipped

serves 4

In a large pot over high heat, combine potatoes, 1 tsp salt, and water to cover by 2 inches and bring to a boil. Cover, reduce heat, and simmer until potatoes are knife-tender, 12–15 minutes.

Drain potatoes thoroughly and return them to empty pot to steam until dry. Once dry, transfer potatoes to a plate or platter. Using a fork, gently crush each potato to flatten and open the top. Top each potato with a bit of crème fraîche, sprinkle with chives, and season with salt and pepper. Transfer to a platter and serve.

Belgian endive was first cultivated by the ancient Egyptians, and today is particularly popular in Belgium and France. We love its easy elegance, crunchy texture, and subtle taste, here paired with spring vegetables and a dash of bright citrus.

grilled asparagus and endive with favas, orange, and mint

CHANGE IT UP

You can substitute English peas for the fava beans, or grilled fennel for the endive. You can also use a broiler instead of a grill to cook the vegetables—just keep a close watch to avoid overcooking them.

SERVE IT WITH

This dish would make a great side for any grilled fish or meat. Pair it with a crisp white wine such as Sauvignon Blanc or Pinot Grigio.

Bring a pot three-fourths full of salted water to a boil over high heat. Meanwhile, prepare a large bowl of ice water. Blanch shucked fava beans in boiling water for 1 minute. Drain and transfer to bowl of ice water. When beans are cool, use your fingers to peel off skins. Set aside.

Preheat a grill to high and oil grill rack. Arrange asparagus and endive slices on grill, making sure they are perpendicular to grate bars and don't fall through grate. (Alternatively, use a grill screen.) Grill, turning occasionally, until evenly charred, 2–3 minutes total. Arrange on a serving platter and season well with salt and pepper.

Using a zester, zest orange over a bowl. Peel and segment orange (page 250), allowing segments and any juices to fall into bowl. Add olive oil and, using a fork, break up orange segments into bite-sized pieces. Season with salt and pepper.

Scatter fava beans and mint on top of grilled vegetables. Drizzle with orange dressing and serve at once.

fava beans 3 lb, outer pods removed

slender asparagus 1 lb, ends trimmed

Belgian endive 2 heads, sliced lengthwise ⅛ inch thick

sea salt and ground pepper

orange 1

extra-virgin olive oil ½ cup

fresh mint ½ cup leaves

serves 4

fritters four ways

fresh corn fritters

stone-ground cornmeal
2 cups

flour 1 Tbsp

baking soda 1 tsp

baking powder 1 tsp

sea salt

green onions ⅓ cup
minced

egg 1, separated, plus
2 egg whites

buttermilk 1½ cups

fresh or thawed frozen
corn kernels 1 cup

fresh chives 1 Tbsp
snipped

vegetable oil for
deep-frying

serves 4–6

In a bowl, combine cornmeal, flour, baking soda, baking powder, and 1 tsp salt and mix well. Add onions, egg yolk, and buttermilk and stir until well combined. Add corn kernels and chives. Using a handheld mixer or a whisk, whip egg whites to stiff peaks. Fold into batter. Set aside.

Pour vegetable oil to a depth of about 2 inches into a large saucepan and heat to 325°F on a deep-frying thermometer. Working in batches to avoid crowding, drop in batter by the tablespoonful and fry until golden brown, 3–5 minutes. Using a slotted spoon, transfer to paper towels to drain. Let oil return to 325°F between batches. Serve hot.

chickpea and paprika fritters

canned chickpeas
1¼ cups

smoked paprika 1 tsp

ground cumin ¼ tsp

serves 4–6

Drain chickpeas well, then crush them with a fork.

Prepare fritter batter as directed (left), substituting chickpeas for corn and paprika and cumin for chives. Fry as directed.

zucchini and mint fritters

zucchini 1½ cups thinly
sliced with a mandoline

sea salt

fresh mint 1 Tbsp
chopped, plus
8–10 leaves for garnish
(optional)

serves 4–6

Sprinkle zucchini with salt and pat dry with paper towels. Prepare fritter batter as directed (above), substituting zucchini for corn kernels and chopped mint for chives. Fry as directed.

Then, if desired, add mint leaves to hot oil and fry until crisp, about 30 seconds. Drain briefly on paper towels, then scatter fried mint leaves over fritters.

broccoli rabe and parmesan fritters

broccoli rabe 1½ cups
chopped

Parmesan cheese ½ cup
freshly grated

serves 4–6

Bring a pot three-fourths full of salted water to a boil over high heat. Meanwhile, prepare a large bowl of ice water. Add broccoli rabe to boiling water and blanch for 1 minute. Drain and transfer to bowl of ice water, then drain again and spread on paper towels to dry.

Prepare fritter batter as directed (above left), substituting blanched broccoli rabe for corn and adding cheese to cornmeal mixture. Fry as directed.

grains four ways

warm farro salad with herbs

extra-virgin olive oil
4 Tbsp

bay leaf 1

fresh rosemary 1 sprig

farro 1 cup

chicken stock 2 cups

sea salt and pepper

grated lemon zest and
juice from 1 lemon

fresh chives, chervil,
flat-leaf parsley, and
green onion ¼ cup
chopped each

fresh tarragon 1½ tsp
chopped

serves 4–6

In a large saucepan over medium heat, warm 2 Tbsp olive oil. Add bay leaf, rosemary, and *farro* and cook, stirring, for 1 minute. Add stock, 2 cups water, 1 tsp salt, and several grinds of pepper. Bring to a boil, then cover, reduce heat, and simmer until *farro* is tender and liquid is absorbed, about 20 minutes. Remove from heat and let cool slightly.

Discard bay leaf and rosemary and transfer *farro* to a bowl. Add lemon zest and juice, 2 Tbsp olive oil, chives, chervil, parsley, green onion, and tarragon and toss to combine. Transfer to a serving dish, sprinkle with salt, and serve warm.

zesty lemon quinoa

quinoa 1 cup

extra-virgin olive oil
4½ tsp

lemon zest 1 tsp grated

fresh lemon juice 2 tsp

fresh flat-leaf parsley
1 Tbsp chopped

pine nuts ¼ cup, toasted

serves 4–6

Rinse quinoa in a bowl of cold water and drain in a fine-mesh sieve. Repeat, rinsing quinoa in a fresh bowl of water and draining again. Fill a pot three-fourths full with salted water and bring to a boil over medium-high heat. Add quinoa and cook, uncovered, until tender, about 20 minutes.

Drain in a fine-mesh sieve and transfer to a bowl. Stir in olive oil, lemon zest and juice, parsley, and pine nuts. Serve warm or at room temperature.

lentils with mustard vinaigrette

Puy lentils 1 cup, picked
over and rinsed

onion 1, finely chopped

garlic 1 clove, halved

dried thyme ¼ tsp

fresh flat-leaf parsley
2 sprigs, plus ½ cup finely
chopped

shallot 1, minced

white wine vinegar 2 tsp

Dijon mustard 4½ tsp

sea salt and ground
pepper

extra-virgin olive oil
¼ cup

serves 4–6

In a heavy saucepan over medium heat, combine lentils, 6 cups water, onion, garlic, thyme, and parsley sprigs. Bring to a simmer, cover, and cook until lentils are tender, about 30 minutes.

Meanwhile, to make vinaigrette, transfer 2 Tbsp lentil-cooking liquid to a bowl and whisk in shallot, vinegar, mustard, and salt and pepper to taste. Whisking constantly, add olive oil in a slow stream until dressing is emulsified.

Drain lentils well in a fine-mesh sieve and discard parsley sprigs and garlic halves. Transfer lentils to a bowl, add vinaigrette and chopped parsley, and toss to combine. Season to taste with salt and pepper and serve warm or at room temperature.

israeli couscous with basil and mint

extra-virgin olive oil
2 Tbsp

red onion 1, finely
chopped

Israeli couscous 1 cup

garlic 1 clove, minced

fresh flat-leaf parsley
½ cup finely chopped

fresh basil ½ cup minced

fresh mint ⅓ cup finely
chopped

fresh lemon juice
1 Tbsp, or to taste

sea salt and ground
pepper

serves 4–6

In a heavy saucepan over medium heat, warm 1 Tbsp olive oil. Add onion and sauté, stirring occasionally, until golden, about 3 minutes. Add couscous and garlic and cook, stirring, for 30 seconds. Add water to cover (about 2 cups) and bring to a boil. Simmer until couscous is al dente, about 15 minutes.

Drain couscous well in a fine-mesh sieve, and transfer to a serving bowl. Fluff couscous with a fork and stir in parsley, basil, mint, lemon juice, and 1 Tbsp olive oil. Season to taste with salt and pepper and serve warm or at room temperature.

Halloumi cheese, which originated in the Mediterranean, is traditionally made with a mixture of goat's and sheep's milk. It's fantastic for grilling, thanks to an unusually high melting temperature (the curds are heated before shaping and brining the cheese).

grilled halloumi with figs and blood oranges

blood oranges 4

fresh mint ½ cup leaves, torn

sea salt and ground pepper

Red or Black Mission figs
6 ripe, halved lengthwise

halloumi cheese ½ lb, cut
into ½-inch-thick slices

extra-virgin olive oil 1½ tsp

serves 4–6

Using a knife, cut off top and bottom of 1 orange and stand it upright. Following contour of fruit, slice off remaining peel and white pith. Holding orange over a bowl, cut along both sides of each segment to separate it from membrane, allowing it and any juices to fall into bowl. Repeat with remaining oranges. Add mint and toss to combine. Season well with salt and pepper. Set aside.

Heat a stove-top grill pan over medium heat. Put figs, skin side down, on grill pan and cook, turning once, until juices start to run, about 2 minutes per side. Add figs to bowl with oranges.

Drizzle cheese slices with olive oil and place on grill pan. Grill, turning once, until golden, 1–2 minutes per side. Add cheese to bowl with oranges. Toss everything together and serve at once.

CHANGE IT UP

Try grilling *halloumi* with other fruits, such as peaches or pineapple. You can also use an outdoor grill instead of a grill pan. Skewers would help to keep the cheese from falling through the grates, and they make for a great serving presentation.

SERVE IT WITH

We love to serve this dish with grilled meat, or with crusty artisanal bread, olives, and a glass of chilled rosé for a lazy afternoon meal. It also works well as a starter.

purée four ways

polenta with fresh corn

sea salt and ground pepper

coarse-grained polenta 1 cup

fresh corn kernels 1 cup (from about 2 ears)

extra-virgin olive oil 3 Tbsp

Parmesan cheese ½ cup freshly grated

serves 4

In a large, heavy saucepan over high heat, bring 4 cups water to a boil. Whisk in 1 tsp salt and polenta, pouring polenta in a slow stream to avoid clumping. Reduce heat to low and cook, stirring frequently, until polenta reaches consistency of thick porridge, about 40 minutes. Add more water if polenta gets too thick.

Stir in corn, cook for 2–3 minutes, then add olive oil and Parmesan and cook just until Parmesan is melted. Season to taste with salt and pepper. Serve at once.

celery root purée

sea salt and ground white pepper

celery roots 2 large, peeled and cut into 2-inch cubes

heavy cream ¼ cup

unsalted butter 4 Tbsp, cut into 5 pieces, at room temperature

serves 4

In a large saucepan, combine 6 cups water and 1 Tbsp salt. Bring just to a boil over high heat, add celery roots, and return to a boil. Reduce heat and simmer until celery roots are tender when pierced with a fork, about 20 minutes. Drain well.

Transfer celery roots to a bowl. Add cream and butter and, using a potato masher, mash until smooth. Season to taste with salt and pepper and serve at once.

polenta with wild mushrooms

sea salt and ground pepper

coarse-grained polenta 1 cup

extra-virgin olive oil 2 Tbsp

garlic 1 clove, minced

fresh thyme 1 tsp minced

wild mushrooms 1 lb, sliced

serves 4

In a large, heavy saucepan over high heat, bring 4 cups water to a boil. Whisk in 1 tsp salt and polenta, pouring polenta in a slow stream to avoid clumping. Reduce heat to low and cook, stirring frequently, until polenta reaches consistency of thick porridge, about 40 minutes. Add more water if polenta gets too thick.

Meanwhile, in a sauté pan over medium heat, warm olive oil. Add garlic and thyme and cook, stirring, until fragrant, about 1 minute. Add mushrooms and sauté, stirring, until mushrooms are tender, about 2 more minutes. Stir cooked mushrooms into polenta and cook for 2–3 minutes. Season to taste with salt and pepper and serve at once.

parsnip purée

parsnips 6–8 medium to large (about 1½ lb total weight), peeled and cut into 1-inch chunks

sea salt and ground pepper

unsalted butter 2 Tbsp, at room temperature

serves 4

In a large saucepan, combine parsnips, 1 Tbsp salt, and 6 cups water. Bring to a boil over medium-high heat and cook until parsnips are tender when pierced with a fork, 20–25 minutes. Drain well.

Transfer parsnips to a food processor, add butter, and purée until smooth. Transfer to a serving bowl, season to taste with salt and pepper, and serve at once.

desserts

In the winter months, it can be hard to find as many fresh ingredients as you'd like. You can always freeze things and then you'll have them on hand when you need them. We love to freeze red currants and use them to garnish desserts—just something extra to make them more special.

italian cheese plate

hard sheep's milk cheese such as pecorino 6–8 oz

blue-veined cheese such as Gorgonzola 6–8 oz

triple-cream cheese such as La Tur 6–8 oz

grapes 1 cup

apricots 4, cut into thin wedges

Marcona almonds ½ cup

serves 4–6

About 2 hours before serving, remove cheeses from refrigerator, unwrap them, and allow them to come to room temperature.

When ready to serve, arrange cheeses, grapes, apricot slices, and almonds on a cutting board, marble slab, or 1 or more platters. Include a spreader for each soft cheese and a sharp paring knife or cheese plane for hard cheese. Offer a bread basket or board with baguette rounds, thin slices of dark bread, or crackers.

farmhouse cheese plate

aged goat's milk cheese 6–8 oz

aged cow's milk cheese such as Gouda or Cheddar 6–8 oz

Gruyère cheese 6–8 oz

apples 2, thinly sliced

apricot chutney ¼ cup

dates ½ cup, pitted

pistachio nuts ½ cup

serves 4–6

About 2 hours before serving, remove cheeses from refrigerator, unwrap them, and allow them to come to room temperature.

When ready to serve, arrange cheeses, apple slices, chutney, dates, and pistachios on a cutting board, marble slab, or 1 or more platters. Include a paring knife or cheese plane for cheeses. Offer a bread basket or board with baguette rounds, thin slices of dark bread, or crackers.

late-harvest cheese plate

....

semisoft blue-veined
cheese such as Blue
Valdeón 6–8 oz

Parmesan cheese
6–8 oz

semihard goat's
milk cheese such as
Garrotxa 6–8 oz

fresh figs 6, quartered

honeycomb ¼ lb

walnuts ½ cup

serves 4–6

About 2 hours before serving, remove
cheeses from refrigerator, unwrap them,
and allow them to come to room temperature.

When ready to serve, arrange cheeses,
figs, honeycomb, and walnuts on a cutting
board, marble slab, or 1 or more platters.
Include a paring knife or cheese plane for
cheeses. Offer a bread basket or board
with baguette rounds, thin slices of dark
bread, or crackers.

winter cheese plate

....

ash-coated goat cheese
such as Humboldt Fog,
Valençay, or Selles-sur-
Cher 6–8 oz

creamy goat's milk
cheese such as crottin
de Chavignol 6–8 oz

Manchego cheese
6–8 oz (optional)

pear 1, thinly sliced

raspberry jam ¼ cup

fig bar 1, sliced

hazelnuts ½ cup, toasted

serves 4–6

About 2 hours before serving, remove
cheeses from refrigerator, unwrap them,
and allow them to come to room temperature.

When ready to serve, arrange cheeses,
pear slices, jam, fig bar, and hazelnuts on
a cutting board, marble slab, or 1 or more
platters. Include a spreader for each soft
cheese and a sharp paring knife or cheese
plane for hard cheeses. Offer a bread
basket or board with baguette rounds,
thin slices of dark bread, or crackers.

This tart takes a bit of work to make, but the result is well worth the effort and is always a crowd-pleaser. It's essential to use a good-quality chocolate with a high cocoa content. Our favorites are Valrhona and Scharffen Berger.

chocolate caramel tart

flour 1¼ cups

unsweetened cocoa
powder ¼ cup

unsalted butter 1 cup,
cut into pieces

powdered sugar ½ cup
plus 1 Tbsp

egg yolk 1

vanilla extract 1 tsp

granulated sugar 2 cups

light corn syrup ¼ cup

heavy cream 2 cups plus
2 Tbsp

semisweet chocolate
10 oz, chopped

fleur de sel for garnish

serves 8

To make a crust, sift flour and cocoa powder together into a bowl. In a stand mixer, beat together ½ cup butter, powdered sugar, egg yolk, and vanilla until just smooth and creamy. Add flour mixture and beat until a dough forms. Do not overwork. Transfer to a work surface, shape into a rectangle, and wrap in plastic wrap. Refrigerate for at least 1 hour or up to overnight. Once dough has chilled, roll it out into a 13-by-10-inch rectangle on a lightly floured work surface. Transfer dough to an 11-by-8-inch tart pan with removable bottom. Press dough into bottom and up sides of pan. Cut off any overhanging dough, and prick dough in several places with a fork. Chill again for at least 30 minutes or up to 1 hour.

Preheat oven to 350°F. Cover dough with parchment paper and fill with pie weights. Bake until sides are cooked through and base is almost cooked through and slightly flaky, 25–30 minutes. Remove pie weights and parchment and continue to cook until the base is dry and set, about 8 minutes. Remove and let cool on a wire rack.

To make a caramel filling, in a saucepan over medium-high heat, combine ½ cup water, granulated sugar, and corn syrup. Cook, stirring occasionally, until sugar turns into a deep amber-colored caramel, about 10 minutes. Remove from heat and, very carefully and slowly, add ½ cup plus 2 Tbsp cream (it will spatter). Add remaining ½ cup butter, 1 piece at a time, stirring until smooth. Pour caramel filling into cooled tart shell, set aside to cool, then chill until firmly set, at least 30 minutes.

To make a chocolate ganache, put chocolate in a heatproof bowl. Bring 1½ cups cream to a boil and pour it over chocolate. Let sit for 2 minutes, then whisk until smooth. Pour over caramel and chill until set, at least 30 minutes. Remove tart from refrigerator 10 minutes before serving. Garnish with *fleur de sel.*

SERVE IT WITH

For a truly decadent pairing, serve this tart with Fleur de Sel Caramel Ice Cream (page 228).

TART PAN VARIATIONS

We like to make this tart in a rectangular tart pan, but you can just as easily make it in a 9-inch round tart pan. Or, if you are feeling adventurous, make tartlets by dividing the crust, caramel filling, and ganache among six 4½-inch round tartlet pans with removable bottoms.

poached fruit four ways

white peaches with lemon verbena

Provençal dry rosé 1 bottle (750 ml)

lemon verbena leaves 10, plus leaves and flowers for garnish

fresh lemon juice from ½ lemon

sugar ½ cup

white peaches 8, peeled, halved, and pitted

serves 6

In a large saucepan over medium-high heat, combine rosé, lemon verbena leaves, lemon juice, and sugar. Bring to a boil, stirring, until sugar dissolves. Add peaches and submerge in liquid. Reduce heat to a gentle simmer and cook until peaches are tender when pierced with a knife, about 10 minutes. Remove from heat and let peaches cool in syrup. Refrigerate until ready to serve.

To serve, place 2 or 3 peach halves in each of 6 small plates, bowls, or glasses. Drizzle with a little syrup, garnish with lemon verbena leaves, and serve at once.

spiced plums

fruity red wine such as Pinot Noir 1 bottle (750 ml)

sugar 1 cup

cloves 3

star anise pods 3

cinnamon sticks 2

fresh ginger 2 thin slices

red plums 2 lb, peeled, pitted, and quartered

Vanilla Mascarpone (page 215)

serves 6

In a large saucepan over medium-high heat, combine wine, sugar, cloves, star anise, cinnamon, and ginger. Bring to a boil. Add plums and reduce heat to low. Cover and simmer until plums are tender, 8–10 minutes.

Using a slotted spoon, transfer plums to a bowl and let cool. Serve in small bowls with vanilla mascarpone.

red wine pears

dry red wine 1 bottle (750 ml)

sugar 1 cup

lemon zest 6 strips, each 1 by 2 inches

star anise pod 1

vanilla bean 1, split lengthwise

Bosc pears 8, firm but ripe, peeled, halved, and cored

serves 6

In a large saucepan, combine wine, sugar, lemon zest, star anise, and 1 cup water. Using the tip of a sharp knife, scrape seeds from vanilla bean into wine mixture. Bring to a boil, stirring until sugar dissolves. Remove from heat.

Add pears, rounded side down, to liquid. Return to a boil, reduce heat to low, cover, and simmer, basting occasionally with cooking liquid, until pears are tender, about 25 minutes. Using a slotted spoon, transfer pears to a bowl.

Strain cooking liquid through a fine-mesh sieve and discard solids. Return cooking liquid to saucepan. Bring to a boil and boil until reduced to 1 cup, about 12 minutes. Pour syrup over pears. Chill for at least 3 hours or up to overnight before serving.

apricots with rose water

vanilla bean 1, split lengthwise

dry rosé wine 1 bottle (750 ml)

sugar 2 cups

lemon zest 5 strips, each 3 by ¾ inch

apricots 10 (about 1¾ lb total weight), halved and pitted

rose water 1 Tbsp

crème fraîche 1 cup

serves 6

Using the tip of a sharp knife, scrape seeds from vanilla bean into a 2-qt saucepan. Add vanilla bean pod, rosé, sugar, and lemon zest. Bring to a boil over medium-high heat, stirring until sugar dissolves. Add apricots, reduce heat to a gentle simmer, and cook, stirring once or twice, until tender, 2–6 minutes, depending on ripeness. Remove from heat and add rose water. Using a slotted spoon, transfer apricots to serving bowls and spoon syrup over top. Top each serving with a dollop of crème fraîche and serve at once.

We first made this recipe with some leftover panettone on the day after Christmas, and we loved it—what a perfect use for that cakelike bread. Also try it with sliced croissants.

mini bread and butter puddings

. . . .

unsalted butter as needed, at room temperature

white bread 8 small slices, ½ inch thick

golden raisins ¼ cup

pine nuts ¼ cup, toasted

milk 1¼ cups

heavy cream ½ cup

light brown sugar ½ cup firmly packed

lemon zest 1 tsp grated

freshly grated nutmeg pinch

eggs 4, lightly beaten

serves 4

Generously butter four 5-inch ramekins or heatproof bowls.

Spread bread with butter, and cut each slice into 8 small triangles. Layer 8 bread triangles in each dish, sprinkle with golden raisins and pine nuts, and top with another 8 bread triangles.

In a bowl, combine milk, cream, brown sugar, lemon zest, and nutmeg and whisk in eggs. Divide mixture among ramekins and leave to soak for 30 minutes. Preheat oven to 350°F.

Place ramekins on a rimmed baking sheet and bake for 30 minutes. Increase oven temperature to 375°F and bake until puddings are crisp and golden on top and just set, about 10 minutes more. Serve at once.

CHANGE IT UP

You can easily vary the ingredients in this basic bread pudding. Substitute currants or dried cherries for the golden raisins, or add in ½ cup semisweet chocolate chips with the raisins and nuts.

SERVE IT WITH

These bread puddings would go great with steaming cups of white hot cocoa (page 235)—a perfect cold-weather combo.

doughnuts with three dipping sauces

mini ricotta doughnuts

canola oil for deep-frying

flour ¾ cup

baking powder 2 tsp

lemon zest 1 tsp grated

salt ¼ tsp

whole-milk ricotta cheese 1 cup

eggs 2, lightly beaten

granulated sugar 2 Tbsp

vanilla extract 1½ tsp

powdered sugar for dusting

dipping sauce of choice (right and below)

makes 24 doughnuts

In a large, heavy saucepan, pour oil to a depth of 1½ inches and heat to 370°F on a deep-frying thermometer.

Meanwhile, in a bowl, whisk together flour, baking powder, lemon zest, and salt. In a large bowl, whisk together ricotta, eggs, granulated sugar, and vanilla. Add flour mixture to ricotta mixture and whisk until well blended.

Working in batches, gently drop level tablespoonfuls of batter into hot oil and fry, turning occasionally, until golden, about 3 minutes. Using a slotted spoon, transfer to paper towels to drain.

Dust with powdered sugar and serve with dipping sauce of choice.

white chocolate sauce

white chocolate 4 oz, coarsely chopped

heavy cream ½ cup

makes about ¾ cup

Put chocolate in top of a double boiler or in a large metal bowl and place it over (but not touching) barely simmering water. Heat, stirring often, until chocolate melts. Remove from heat and set aside.

In a small saucepan over medium heat, heat cream until very hot but not quite simmering. Whisk hot cream into melted chocolate until smooth. Use at once, or cover and refrigerate until ready to use. Warm gently in top of a double boiler before using.

dark chocolate sauce

dark chocolate 4 oz, coarsely chopped

heavy cream ½ cup

makes about ¾ cup

Put chocolate in top of a double boiler or in a large metal bowl and place it over (but not touching) barely simmering water. Heat, stirring often, until chocolate melts. Remove from heat and set aside.

In a small saucepan over medium heat, heat cream until very hot but not quite simmering. Whisk hot cream into melted chocolate until smooth. Use at once, or cover and refrigerate until ready to use. Warm gently in top of a double boiler before using.

caramel sauce

sugar ½ cup

unsalted butter 1 Tbsp, cut into small pieces

heavy cream ¼ cup

makes about ¾ cup

Put sugar in a heavy saucepan and add enough water just to cover sugar (it will resemble wet sand). Place over medium-high heat and cook, without stirring, but swirling pan occasionally to ensure even cooking, until mixture starts to bubble and edges begin to turn amber, 7–10 minutes. Watching carefully to prevent overcooking, continue cooking until mixture turns a deep amber, 3–5 minutes more. Remove from heat and very carefully add butter (it may spatter). Carefully add cream and swirl pan until mixture is evenly mixed.

Use at once, or cover and refrigerate until ready to use. Warm gently in top of a double boiler before using.

The evocative Middle Eastern flavors of pistachios, citrus, honey, and mint are perfect with ricotta. When combined, they make a subtly sweet but tangy dessert—and a great finish to a spicy meal like our grilled kebabs (page 149).

oranges with fresh ricotta and pistachios

. . . .

blood oranges 4

oranges, preferably Cara Cara 4

orange flower water 2 tsp

fresh ricotta cheese 2 cups

pistachio nuts ½ cup chopped

honey ½ cup

fresh mint handful of sprigs, for garnish

serves 8

Using a knife, cut off top and bottom of each orange and stand it upright. Following contour of fruit, slice off remaining peel and white pith. In a shallow bowl, cut each orange crosswise into ¼-inch-thick rounds, capturing any juice released in bowl. Add orange flower water to orange juice.

Arrange 5 or 6 orange slices in each of 8 clear glass bowls or small plates, placing them to one side. Place ¼ cup ricotta along opposite side. Sprinkle with 1 Tbsp pistachios, drizzle with 1 Tbsp honey, garnish with a mint sprig, and serve at once.

CHANGE IT UP

You can swap out the pistachios for another type of nut. Roasted almonds or cashews would work well. Make sure they aren't salted or they will throw off the balance of the other flavors in the dish.

PAIR IT WITH

A mint tea or a lemon-verbena tisane would be the perfect accompaniment to this light and refreshing dessert. Or, since it's not too sweet, try a dessert wine, like Italian *vin santo*.

strawberry millefeuille

puff pastry 1 sheet (½ package), thawed according to package directions and unfolded

egg 1, lightly beaten

strawberries 1½ cups thinly sliced

fresh lemon juice from ½ lemon

granulated sugar 1 Tbsp

heavy cream 1 cup

powdered sugar for dusting

serves 6

Preheat oven to 375°F. On a lightly floured board, roll out pastry sheet to a ¼-inch thickness. Cut in half lengthwise. Transfer the 2 rectangles to a rimmed baking sheet. Prick them evenly all over with a fork and brush with beaten egg. Bake until puffed and golden, about 20 minutes.

Meanwhile, in a bowl, combine strawberries, lemon juice, and sugar and stir to combine. Set aside. In another bowl, using a whisk, whip cream until it forms soft peaks.

With a serrated knife, slice 1 rectangle horizontally to create 2 layers. Use uncut rectangle as base. Top with half of whipped cream and one-third of berries. Repeat with remaining ingredients to create 2 more layers, finishing with just berries. Dust with powdered sugar just before serving.

blueberry-lime ginger tartlets

gingersnap cookies 10 oz (about 30–40 cookies), coarsely broken

unsalted butter 6 Tbsp, melted

Lime Curd (page 219) 1 cup

blueberries 2½ cups

lime 1

powdered sugar for dusting

serves 4

Preheat oven to 350°F. In a food processor, grind gingersnaps to fine crumbs. Transfer to a bowl and add melted butter. Stir until thoroughly combined. Press mixture evenly into bottoms and sides of 4 tartlet pans with removable bottoms, each 4¾ inches in diameter. Bake until crusts are a deep gold, about 12 minutes. Transfer to a wire rack and let cool completely.

Remove tartlet shells from pans and fill with curd. Top with blueberries. Finely grate zest from lime and sprinkle over tartlets. Add a squeeze of lime juice over each tartlet. Dust with powdered sugar just before serving.

cherries with vanilla mascarpone

Rainier cherries 1½ lb

mascarpone cheese 1 cup

vanilla extract 1 tsp

sugar 1 tsp

ice cubes

serves 4–6

Place cherries in a serving bowl. In a separate bowl, stir together mascarpone, vanilla, and sugar. Transfer to a small serving bowl. Add ice to bowl of cherries. Serve mascarpone mixture alongside.

mixed berries with sabayon

mixed berries 2 cups

egg yolks 4, at room temperature

lemon zest from 1 lemon, grated

granulated sugar ¼ cup, plus 2 Tbsp

dessert wine such as Muscat ¾ cup, at room temperature

powdered sugar for dusting

serves 6

Fill a bowl three-fourths full with ice water and set aside. Pour 2 inches water into a saucepan and bring to a gentle boil. Meanwhile, divide berries among 6 small ovenproof plates or ramekins.

In a large stainless-steel bowl, whisk together egg yolks, lemon zest, and sugar until pale and slightly thickened, about 2 minutes. Add wine. Set bowl over the gently boiling water and whisk constantly until sabayon is thick and has doubled in volume, about 8 minutes. Immediately set bowl in ice-water bath.

Preheat broiler. Spoon sabayon evenly over berries. Place plates on a rimmed baking sheet and broil until sabayon is golden, about 3 minutes. Remove from oven and dust with powdered sugar. Serve at once.

We use these meringues to make an Eton mess, a popular dessert in England. It's simple to make and fun to eat! Layer the meringues in a large, shallow bowl with whipped cream and a fruit curd (page 219). Our favorite is passion fruit.

meringues

· ·

CHANGE UP THE FLAVOR

While we enjoy the simplicity and elegance of these classic meringues just as they are, many people like to flavor them. You can fold toasted flaked coconut or chopped nuts into the stiff egg whites, or replace the vanilla extract with finely grated citrus zest or a spice such as ground cardamom. For a Christmas treat, you can sprinkle them with crushed candy canes just before baking.

SERVE IT WITH

Delicate meringues are the perfect ending to a long, heavy meal. They are lovely served with sliced fresh fruit and a cup of tea.

Preheat oven to 275°F. Line 2 rimmed baking sheets with parchment paper.

In a stand mixer fitted with whisk attachment, combine egg whites, salt, and cream of tartar and whip on medium speed until egg whites are opaque and just holding their shape. Increase speed to medium-high and add sugar, 1 Tbsp at a time. When egg whites form stiff, glossy peaks, whip in vanilla extract.

To shape each meringue, scoop 2 Tbsp of whipped egg whites onto prepared baking sheets. Bake until crisp but not colored, about 30 minutes. Turn off oven and let cool completely in oven.

To serve, arrange meringues on a platter and sprinkle with sugar.

egg whites 4

salt 1 pinch

cream of tartar ⅛ tsp

superfine sugar ¾ cup, plus more for sprinkling

vanilla extract 1 tsp

serves 4–6

fruit curd four ways

passion fruit curd

sugar ¾ cup

eggs 2 whole, plus
4 egg yolks

unsalted butter ½ cup
cold, cut into small pieces

passion fruit juice
½ cup, strained

fresh lime juice from
1 lime

passion fruit seeds from
1 passion fruit

**makes about
1½ cups**

In a bowl, whisk together sugar, whole eggs, and egg yolks. In a saucepan over low heat, combine butter and passion fruit and lime juices. Warm, stirring, until butter melts. Add egg mixture to saucepan and cook, stirring constantly, until mixture has thickened and coats the back of a wooden spoon, 5–8 minutes.

Remove from heat and transfer curd to a small heatproof container. Cover with plastic wrap, pressing it onto surface, and refrigerate until ready to serve. Let come to room temperature before using. Stir in passion fruit seeds just before serving.

lime curd

sugar 1 cup

eggs 2 whole, plus
4 egg yolks

unsalted butter ½ cup
cold, cut into small pieces

fresh lime juice ½ cup
plus 2 Tbsp

lime zest 1 tsp grated

**makes about
1½ cups**

In a bowl, whisk together sugar, whole eggs, and egg yolks. In a saucepan over low heat, combine butter and lime juice. Warm, stirring, until butter melts. Add egg mixture to saucepan and cook, stirring constantly, until mixture has thickened and coats the back of a wooden spoon, about 5 minutes.

Remove from heat and transfer curd to a small heatproof container. Cover with plastic wrap, pressing it onto surface, and refrigerate until ready to serve. Let come to room temperature before using. Stir in zest just before serving.

meyer lemon curd

sugar ¾ cup

eggs 2 whole, plus
4 egg yolks

unsalted butter ½ cup
cold, cut into small pieces

fresh Meyer lemon juice
½ cup plus 2 Tbsp

Meyer lemon zest 2 tsp
grated

**makes about
1½ cups**

In a bowl, whisk together sugar, whole eggs, and egg yolks. In a saucepan over low heat, combine butter and lemon juice. Warm, stirring, until butter melts. Add egg mixture to saucepan and cook, stirring constantly, until mixture has thickened and coats the back of a wooden spoon, about 5 minutes.

Remove from heat and transfer curd to a small heatproof container. Cover with plastic wrap, pressing it onto surface, and refrigerate until ready to serve. Let come to room temperature before using. Stir in zest just before serving.

tangerine curd

sugar ¾ cup

eggs 2 whole, plus
4 egg yolks

unsalted butter ½ cup
cold, cut into small pieces

fresh tangerine juice
½ cup plus 2 Tbsp

tangerine zest 1 tsp
grated

**makes about
1½ cups**

In a bowl, whisk together sugar, whole eggs, and egg yolks. In a saucepan over low heat, combine butter and tangerine juice. Warm, stirring constantly, until butter melts. Add egg mixture to saucepan and cook, stirring constantly, until mixture has thickened and coats the back of a wooden spoon, about 5 minutes.

Remove from heat and transfer curd to a small heatproof container. Cover with plastic wrap, pressing it onto surface, and refrigerate until ready to serve. Let come to room temperature before using. Stir in zest just before serving.

fruit crumble four ways

blackberry and apple crumble

flour 1¾ cups

sugar 1½ cups

fine sea salt 1 tsp

unsalted butter 1 cup
cold, cut into 1-inch cubes

rolled oats 1 cup

blackberries 2 pints

apples 3 lb peeled,
cored, and sliced

Lemon Cream (page
224) or whipped cream
for serving (optional)

serves 6-8

Preheat oven to 375°F. To make topping, in a food processor, pulse 1½ cups flour, ¾ cup sugar, and salt until combined. Add butter and pulse until mixture resembles coarse bread crumbs. Add oats and pulse to combine. Transfer to a bowl.

To make fruit filling, in a bowl, combine blackberries, apples, ¾ cup sugar, and ¼ cup flour.

Spread fruit filling in a 9-by-13-inch baking dish. Using your fingers, press topping into large clumps and scatter over fruit. Bake until fruit is bubbling and topping is golden and crisp, about 1 hour. Alternatively, divide fruit and topping among eight ½-cup ramekins and bake for 30 minutes. Serve warm or at room temperature with whipped cream (if using).

apricot and raspberry crumble

crumble topping
(left)

apricots 3 lb, pitted and
sliced

raspberries 2 pints

sugar ¾ cup

flour ¼ cup

serves 6-8

Prepare crumble topping as directed.

To make fruit filling, in a bowl, combine apricots, raspberries, sugar, and flour.

Spread fruit filling in a 9-by-13-inch baking dish. Using your fingers, press topping into large clumps and scatter over fruit. Bake until fruit is bubbling and topping is golden and crisp, about 1 hour. Alternatively, divide fruit and topping among eight ½-cup ramekins and bake for 30 minutes. Serve warm or at room temperature.

plum, lime, and ginger crumble

. . . .

crumble topping
(far left)

red plums 3½ lb, pitted and sliced

crystallized ginger
1 cup chopped

lime zest from 2 limes, grated

sugar ¾ cup

flour ¼ cup

vanilla ice cream for serving (optional)

serves 6–8

Prepare crumble topping as directed.

To make fruit filling, in a bowl, combine plums, ginger, lime zest, sugar, and flour.

Spread fruit filling in a 9-by-13-inch baking dish. Using your fingers, press topping into large clumps and scatter over fruit. Bake until fruit is bubbling and topping is golden and crisp, about 1 hour. Alternatively, divide fruit and topping among eight ½-cup ramekins and bake for 30 minutes. Serve warm or at room temperature with ice cream (if using).

strawberry and rhubarb crumble

. . . .

crumble topping
(far left)

rhubarb 2 lb, strings removed and sliced on diagonal into ½-inch-thick slices

strawberries 4 pints, sliced

sugar ¾ cup

flour ¼ cup

serves 6–8

Prepare crumble topping as directed.

To make fruit filling, in a bowl, combine rhubarb, strawberries, sugar, and flour.

Spread fruit filling in a 9-by-13-inch baking dish. Using your fingers, press topping into large clumps and scatter over fruit. Bake until fruit is bubbling and topping is golden and crisp, about 1 hour. Alternatively, divide fruit and topping among eight ½-cup ramekins and bake for 30 minutes. Serve warm or at room temperature.

rosé champagne granita

....

sugar ½ cup
rosé Champagne
1 bottle (750 ml)
fresh lime juice 1 Tbsp

serves 6–8

In a saucepan, stir together sugar and 1½ cups water. Bring to a boil over medium-high heat, stirring occasionally until sugar has completely dissolved. Once mixture has come to a boil, remove from heat and let cool. When mixture has cooled completely, stir in Champagne and lime juice.

Pour mixture into a shallow freezer-safe container. Freeze for about 1 hour, then, using a fork, scrape and stir to break up ice crystals. Return granita to freezer until firm, 8–12 hours, occasionally scraping and stirring with a fork.

To serve, spoon granita into small chilled glasses or bowls and serve at once.

sauternes and lemon honey granita

....

honey 6 Tbsp
Sauternes 1 bottle
(750 ml)
grated lemon zest and juice from 1 lemon
edible flowers for garnish (optional)

serves 6–8

In a saucepan, stir together honey and 1½ cups water. Bring to a boil over high heat, reduce to a simmer, and simmer, stirring occasionally, until honey has completely dissolved. Once mixture has returned to a boil, remove from heat and let cool. When mixture has cooled completely, stir in Sauternes and lemon zest and juice.

Pour mixture into a shallow freezer-safe container. Freeze for about 1 hour, then, using a fork, scrape and stir to break up ice crystals. Return granita to freezer until firm, 8–12 hours, occasionally scraping and stirring with a fork.

To serve, spoon granita into small chilled glasses or bowls and serve at once. Garnish with edible flowers (if using).

espresso granita

dark brown sugar
½ cup firmly packed

brewed espresso
4½ cups, hot

Frangelico as needed
(optional)

serves 6–8

In a bowl, combine brown sugar and espresso and stir until sugar is dissolved. Let cool completely. If desired, add Frangelico, 1 Tbsp at a time, to taste.

Pour mixture into a shallow freezer-safe container. Freeze for about 30 minutes, then, using a fork, scrape and stir to break up ice crystals. Return granita to freezer until firm, 8–12 hours, occasionally scraping and stirring with a fork.

To serve, spoon granita into small chilled glasses or bowls and serve at once.

red wine and orange granita

sugar ½ cup

**fruity red wine such as
Pinot Noir** 1 bottle
(750 ml)

fresh orange juice from
1 orange

edible flowers for
garnish (optional)

serves 6–8

In a saucepan, stir together sugar and 1 cup water. Bring to a boil over medium-high heat, stirring occasionally until sugar has completely dissolved. Once mixture has come to a boil, remove from heat and let cool. When mixture has cooled completely, stir in wine and orange juice.

Pour mixture into a shallow freezer-safe container. Freeze for about 1 hour, then, using a fork, scrape and stir to break up ice crystals. Return granita to freezer until firm, 8–12 hours, occasionally scraping and stirring with a fork.

To serve, spoon granita into small chilled glasses or bowls and serve at once. Garnish with edible flowers (if using).

winter compote with three flavored creams

winter compote

. . . .

dry white wine 1 bottle
(750 ml)

honey ¼ cup

cinnamon stick 1

star anise pod 1

Bosc pears 4, peeled,
cored, and sliced ½ inch
thick

Granny Smith apples
4, peeled, cored, and
sliced ½ inch thick

kumquats 16, sliced
⅛ inch thick

dried Kalamata figs
1 lb (about 16), quartered

flavored cream
of choice (right and
below) for serving

serves 8

In a large saucepan over medium-high heat,
combine wine, honey, cinnamon stick, and
star anise. Bring to a boil, stirring occasionally
to combine all ingredients. Add pears,
apples, kumquats, and figs. Reduce heat
to medium-low and simmer until apples
are just tender when pierced with a knife,
5–7 minutes.

Remove from heat and let cool. Remove
and discard cinnamon stick. Refrigerate
until ready to serve. Serve with flavored
cream of choice.

lemon cream

. . . .

lemon zest from
2 Meyer lemons, grated

superfine sugar ¼ cup

heavy cream 2 cups

serves 8

Set 1 tsp lemon zest aside for garnish. In
a small bowl, combine remaining lemon
zest and sugar, rubbing sugar and zest
between your fingertips to combine lemon
oils with sugar. Using a stand mixer fitted
with whisk attachment, whip cream on
medium-high speed just until it starts to
thicken. Gradually add lemon sugar and
whip until combined.

Scoop cream into a serving bowl, sprinkle
with reserved lemon zest, and serve.

cinnamon cream

. . . .

heavy cream 2 cups

superfine sugar ¼ cup

Goldschlager cinnamon
liquor 1 Tbsp

ground cinnamon 1 tsp,
plus more for garnish

serves 8

Using a stand mixer fitted with whisk
attachment, whip together heavy cream,
sugar, cinnamon liquor, and ground
cinnamon on high speed until cream
just starts to thicken.

Scoop cream into a serving bowl, sprinkle
with a pinch of ground cinnamon, and
serve at once.

mascarpone and honey cream

. . . .

mascarpone cheese
2 cups

honey 4 Tbsp, plus
1 Tbsp for drizzling

orange flower water
½ Tbsp

serves 8

Put mascarpone in a bowl. Lightly whisk
in 4 Tbsp honey. Add orange flower water
and whisk to combine.

Place in a small serving bowl and drizzle
with 1 Tbsp honey. Serve at once.

Our good friend Lora Zarubin makes this delicious cake for ginger lovers like us. Avoid woody, dry ginger. Instead, always look for young, moist ginger, which will impart a zippy flavor.

citrus-ginger cake with orange liqueur glaze

flour 1½ cups

baking soda 1 tsp

salt ¼ tsp

unsalted butter ½ cup

heavy cream ¼ cup

dark brown sugar 1 cup firmly packed

dark molasses ½ cup

eggs 3

fresh ginger ⅓ cup finely grated

orange zest 2 Tbsp grated

Cointreau ½ cup

candied orange zest for garnish

serves 8

Preheat oven to 350°F. Butter and flour a 9-inch springform pan, tapping out excess flour.

In a bowl, sift together flour, baking soda, and salt. Set aside.

In a small saucepan over low heat, combine butter and cream and heat gently until butter is melted. Remove from heat and set aside.

Using a stand mixer fitted with paddle attachment, beat together ½ cup brown sugar and molasses on medium speed until well blended. Add eggs, one at a time, beating well after each addition. On medium-low speed, slowly pour cream mixture into brown sugar mixture, followed by flour mixture. Mix until well combined. Stir in ginger and orange zest.

Pour batter into prepared pan. Bake until just cooked through and a thin skewer inserted into middle of cake comes out clean, 25–30 minutes. Do not overcook or cake will become dry. Release and lift off pan sides, and slide cake off pan bottom onto a wire rack. Let cool completely.

Transfer cake to a serving plate. To make glaze, in a small saucepan over medium heat, combine ½ cup brown sugar and Cointreau and heat, stirring occasionally, until sugar has dissolved. Remove from heat and brush glaze on top of cake. Allow cake to rest for 1–2 hours. Garnish with candied orange zest and serve.

CHANGE IT UP

We make our glaze with orange liqueur, but you could easily substitute any flavored liqueur you like.

ON THE SIDE

Moist and rich, this cake is great on its own, though few guests will turn down a dollop of vanilla ice cream or whipped cream on their plate.

Rich and decadent, this is Alison's dream dessert. The added savory crunch from the sea salt is out of this world! Sea salt caramels originated in Brittany, France, where bakers used the local salted butter to make the caramel, and then sprinkled locally harvested *fleur de sel* on top.

fleur de sel caramel ice cream

DRESS IT UP

We like to serve this ice cream between thin ginger or chocolate cookies for a sophisticated version of an ice cream sandwich. Place a scoop of slightly softened ice cream on a cookie, then top with another cookie and gently press them together to flatten the ice cream evenly. Place the sandwiches in the freezer in individual resealable bags or a freezer-safe container for at least 1 hour or up to 1 week before serving.

In a saucepan over medium-high heat, combine milk and cream and bring to a boil. Remove from heat and set aside. In a heavy, deep saucepan over medium-high heat, cook sugar until it begins to melt around the edges, about 5 minutes. Continue to cook, stirring with a wooden spoon, until sugar has melted and turned a dark amber, 3–5 minutes more. Carefully add butter, then pour reserved milk-and-cream mixture down side of pan in a slow, steady stream, stirring constantly. Reduce heat to medium and continue to cook, carefully stirring, until caramel is completely melted and mixture has returned to a bare simmer. Remove caramel mixture from heat and set aside.

Fill a bowl three-fourths full with ice water and set aside. In a bowl, vigorously whisk together egg yolks and vanilla until mixture turns pale and volume has doubled, about 2 minutes. Whisking constantly, slowly add caramel mixture to egg mixture and whisk until smooth. Pour mixture back into saucepan and place over medium heat. Cook, stirring constantly with a wooden spoon, until custard is thick enough to coat back of spoon or until it registers 175°F on a candy thermometer, 1–2 minutes. Do not let it boil. Remove from heat and immediately pour hot custard through a fine-mesh sieve into a heatproof bowl.

Immediately set bowl in ice-water bath and stir custard occasionally until cool. Remove custard from ice bath, cover, and refrigerate until very cold, at least 3 hours or up to overnight.

Pour custard into an ice-cream maker and freeze according to manufacturer's instructions. Transfer ice cream to a freezer-safe container and stir in *fleur de sel*. Press a piece of parchment paper onto surface of ice cream and freeze until firm, at least 2 hours or up to 1 week, before serving.

milk 4 cups

heavy cream 2 cups

sugar 3 cups

unsalted butter ½ cup

egg yolks 12

vanilla extract 2 tsp

fleur de sel 1¼ tsp

makes about 2 qt

Alison grew up with these delicious pink-frosted cupcakes, commonly known in England as fairy or butterfly cakes. Nowadays, friends request these pretty confections—all the time it seems—for baby showers and other celebrations.

rose and vanilla cupcakes

. . . .

self-rising flour 1½ cups

salt 2 pinches

unsalted butter 1¼ cups, at room temperature

granulated sugar ¾ cup

rose water 4½ tsp plus 1 Tbsp

vanilla extract 2½ tsp

eggs 3, lightly beaten

powdered sugar 3 cups, sifted, plus more for dusting (optional)

pink food coloring 3 drops

pistachio nuts 2 Tbsp finely chopped

makes 12 cupcakes

Preheat oven to 350°F. Line a 12-cup muffin pan with paper liners.

Sift flour and 1 pinch of salt into a small bowl and set aside.

In a stand mixer fitted with paddle attachment, beat together ¾ cup butter and granulated sugar on medium-high speed until light and fluffy, scraping down sides of bowl as necessary. Add 4½ tsp rose water and 1½ tsp vanilla. On medium speed, add eggs, one at a time, scraping down sides of bowl and making sure each egg is fully incorporated before adding the next one. On low speed, gradually add flour mixture, mixing until just incorporated.

Divide mixture evenly among prepared muffin cups. Bake until golden and a skewer inserted in the center of a cupcake comes out clean, 15–20 minutes. Let cool completely on a wire rack.

While cupcakes are cooling, make buttercream. In the stand mixer fitted with paddle attachment, beat together ½ cup butter, 3 cups powdered sugar, and 1 pinch salt until smooth. Mix in 1 Tbsp rose water, 1 tsp vanilla, and a few drops food coloring. Place buttercream in a pastry bag fitted with a star tip.

To decorate as fairy cakes, using a small paring knife, cut a cone-shaped piece from the top of each cupcake. Each cone should be about 1½ inches in diameter and about 1 inch long. Cut each cone in half lengthwise. These 2 pieces will be "wings" for each fairy cake. Pipe buttercream into center and over top of each cupcake. Insert wings in center, poking tips into frosting and turning flat side of each piece outward. Sprinkle cakes with pistachios, dust with powdered sugar (if using), and serve.

VARY THE PRESENTATION

Fairy dusted Garnish with pretty sprinkles or dragées.

Mini loaves To make mini loaves, use 4 well-greased mini loaf pans with 4-by-2-inch bases in place of muffin pan. Stir ½ cup chopped pistachios into batter just before pouring into loaf pans. Bake at 325°F until a skewer inserted into the centers comes out clean, 40–45 minutes. Turn loaves out of pans onto a wire rack and let cool. Frost with buttercream and garnish with additional pistachios.

Topped with roses Wingless fairy cakes can be topped with small fresh roses (make sure they are pesticide free) or candied rose petals. Wrap cakes with the trimmed edge of a doily.

Truffles are easy to prepare and can be stored in the freezer (well wrapped) for at least 3 months. They are also fun to make—sitting around chatting and rolling can be quite relaxing. Listen to the Beatles' song "Savoy Truffle" as you make them!

chocolate truffles

VARY THE FLAVOR

Toasted coconut Replace cocoa powder with ½ cup flaked coconut, toasted.

Cinnamon sugar Replace cocoa powder with 1 Tbsp ground cinnamon mixed into ½ cup sugar.

Praline Replace cocoa powder with ½ cup finely chopped peanut brittle.

Pink peppercorn After rolling truffles in cocoa powder, gently press a small pinch of finely ground pink peppercorns into top of each truffle.

Sea salt After rolling truffles in cocoa powder, gently press a small pinch of Maldon or other flaky sea salt into top of each truffle.

In a saucepan over medium-high heat, heat cream until very hot but not quite simmering. Remove from heat and stir in chocolate and butter until they are melted and mixture is smooth. Add brandy and whisk until a smooth ganache forms. Transfer to a bowl, cover, and refrigerate until firm, about 1 hour.

Line a rimmed baking sheet with parchment paper. Scoop level tablespoonfuls of chilled ganache and place on prepared baking sheet. Chill for 10 minutes. Spread cocoa powder on a plate. Using your hands, shape each tablespoonful of ganache into a ball or a log 1½ inches long. Roll in cocoa powder and return to baking sheet.

Return truffles to refrigerator for at least 30 minutes to firm. Remove them from refrigerator 20 minutes before serving.

heavy cream 1 cup

semisweet chocolate 12 oz, finely chopped

unsalted butter 4 Tbsp, at room temperature

brandy 1 Tbsp

unsweetened cocoa powder ½ cup

makes 4 dozen truffles

white hot cocoa four ways

madagascan white cocoa

white chocolate 4 oz, chopped

vanilla extract ½ tsp

milk 1¾ cups

heavy cream ¼ cup

star anise pods 3

serves 4

Place white chocolate and vanilla in a heatproof bowl. In a saucepan over medium-high heat, combine milk, cream, and star anise and heat just to a simmer. Pour milk mixture through a fine-mesh sieve over white chocolate. Whisk until chocolate has melted and mixture is smooth. Pour into mugs and serve.

cardamom-clove white cocoa

white chocolate 4 oz, chopped

vanilla extract ½ tsp

milk 1¾ cups

heavy cream ¼ cup

cinnamon stick 1

cloves 4

cardamom pods 3

ground cinnamon for garnish (optional)

serves 4

Place white chocolate and vanilla in a heatproof bowl. In a saucepan over medium-high heat, combine milk, cream, cinnamon stick, cloves, and cardamom and heat just to a simmer. Remove from heat and let stand for 2 minutes. Pour milk mixture through a fine-mesh sieve over white chocolate. Whisk until chocolate has melted and mixture is smooth. Pour into mugs, garnish with ground cinnamon (if using), and serve.

moroccan white cocoa

white chocolate 4 oz, chopped

milk 1¾ cups

heavy cream ¼ cup

mint tea 1 tea bag

serves 4

Place white chocolate in a heatproof bowl. In a saucepan over medium-high heat, combine milk and cream and heat just to a simmer. Remove from heat, add tea bag, and let steep for 2 minutes. Remove tea bag and pour milk mixture over white chocolate. Whisk until chocolate has melted and mixture is smooth. Pour into mugs and serve.

english lavender white cocoa

dried lavender flowers 1 Tbsp

white chocolate 4 oz, chopped

vanilla extract ½ tsp

milk 1¾ cups

heavy cream ¼ cup

serves 4

Wrap lavender in a piece of cheesecloth and tie tightly closed with kitchen string. Combine white chocolate and vanilla in a heatproof bowl. In a saucepan over medium-high heat, combine milk and cream and heat just to a simmer. Remove from heat, add lavender, and let steep for 2 minutes. Pour milk mixture through a fine-mesh sieve over white chocolate. Whisk until chocolate has melted and mixture is smooth. Pour into mugs and serve.

inspired by **spring**

We have an embarrassing secret. Sometimes we throw a dinner party just to get some help in eating all of the marvelous and fresh but excessive purchases we've made at the farmers' market. It's not that we don't find the company of our friends its own reward. But in spring, with so many new crops filling the market bins, we always get a little carried away.

FRUITS
avocados
black currants
blood oranges
blueberries
dried currants
grapefruits
kiwifruits
kumquats
lemons
limes
mangoes
Meyer lemons
navel oranges
papayas
pears
pineapples
prunes
raisins
red currants
strawberries

VEGETABLES
asparagus
artichokes
broccoli
broccoli rabe
butter lettuce
cabbage
carrots
cauliflower
celery
chanterelle mushrooms
endive
English peas
fava beans
fennel
fingerling potatoes
green beans
green bell peppers
haricots verts
jicama
leeks
mâche
morel mushrooms
new potatoes
pea shoots
purslane
radishes
rhubarb
shallots
shiitake mushrooms
snow peas
sorrel
spinach
spring onions
sugar snap peas
Swiss chard
watercress

HERBS
borage
chervil
chives
cilantro
dill
ginger
lemon thyme
parsley
tarragon
thyme

FLOWERS
cherry blossoms
daffodils
delphiniums
hyacinths
irises
narcissus
peonies
pussywillows
ranunculus
sweet peas
tulips

inspired by **summer**

Summer is the most glorious season for fresh fruits, including tomatoes, a fruit to us. It's hard *not* to make a gorgeous meal out of the bright, ripe, and flavorful bounty. As we whiz along on our way to the beach, we like to pull over at farm stands, and then cook that night whatever we bought there and invite the neighbors to dinner.

FRUITS	VEGETABLES	HERBS	FLOWERS
apricots	arugula	basil	chrysanthemums
avocados	beet greens	chives	coreopsis
blackberries	bell peppers	cilantro	cornflowers
black currants	carrots	garlic	cosmos
blueberries	chiles	ginger	daisies
cantaloupes	corn	lavender	delphiniums
cherries	cranberry beans	lemon verbena	forget-me-nots
dates	cucumbers	marjoram	freesias
figs	eggplants	mint	gerbera daisies
green mangoes	fingerling potatoes	oregano	hydrangeas
honeydew melons	green beans	parsley	lisianthus
limes	haricots verts	rosemary	nasturtiums
mangoes	Italian (romano) beans	sage	Oriental lilies
nectarines	lettuce	summer savory	pansies
papayas	okra	tarragon	poppies
passion fruits	Padrón peppers	thyme	Queen Anne's lace
peaches	purslane		roses
pineapples	sorrel		snapdragons
plums	sugar snap peas		sunflowers
Pluots	summer squashes		tuberoses
raspberries	wax beans		zinnias
tomatillos	zucchini		
tomatoes	zucchini flowers		
Valencia oranges			
watermelons			

casual dinner
4

TO START

spring radishes with butter
and sea salt, 50

THE MEAL

provençal mussels, 134

butter lettuce salad with
fresh herbs, 94

crusty bread

TO FINISH

meringues, 216

TO DRINK

white wine / Sauvignon Blanc

red wine / Sangiovese

casual dinner
4

TO START

farmhouse cheese plate, 202

THE MEAL

poached chicken soup with
lemon and spinach, 85

slow-roasted tomatoes, 179

crusty bread

TO FINISH

strawberry and rhubarb
crumble, 221

TO DRINK

white wine / Vermentino

red wine / Zinfandel

casual dinner
6

TO START

shrimp and mâche
salad, 63

THE MEAL

roasted chicken with spring
herbs, 145

white wine and tarragon
sauce, 146

zesty lemon quinoa, 192

TO FINISH

espresso granita, 223

TO DRINK

white wine / Pinot Blanc

red wine / Côtes du Rhône

casual dinner
8

TO START

vignole soup, 82

THE MEAL

slow-roasted salmon, 133

grilled leeks with
romesco, 53

new potatoes with crème
fraîche, 187

TO FINISH

blueberry-lime ginger
tartlets, 214

TO DRINK

white wine / Chardonnay

red wine / Pinot Noir

---

spring menus

---

elegant dinner
4

TO START

wild salmon crudo with
lemon and mint, 69

THE MEAL

roasted lamb chops with
gremolata, 165

roasted fingerlings with
garlic, 186

mâche, purslane, and green
onion salad, 95

TO FINISH

strawberry millefeuille, 214

TO DRINK

aperitif / fruity bellini, 37

white wine / White Burgundy

red wine / Rioja

elegant dinner
8

TO START

chilled spring pea soup
with mint, 86

THE MEAL

sole en papillote, 130

pea and asparagus salad with
meyer lemon dressing, 110

TO FINISH

mini ricotta doughnuts with
caramel dipping sauce, 210

TO DRINK

white wine / French Chardonnay

red wine / Cabernet Sauvignon

cocktail party
8

TO DRINK

orange blossom gin fizz, 22

elder flower white
cosmopolitan, 26

TO PASS

fava, goat cheese, and mint
crostini, 75

shrimp cocktail, 62

italian cheese plate, 202

cocktail party
12

TO DRINK

spring white sangria, 25

lillet lemon, 17

TO PASS

crudités with tzatziki, 49

fritto misto, 60

prosciutto and arugula
flatbread, 72

casual dinner
4

TO START
grilled padrón peppers with
sea salt, 46

THE MEAL
citrus-soaked squid
kebabs, 137

tomato, melon, and
pepita salad, 178

fresh corn fritters, 191

TO FINISH
apricots with rose water, 206

TO DRINK
white wine / Sauvignon Blanc

red wine / Bordeaux

casual dinner
4

TO START
avocado, basil, and tomato
crostini, 74

THE MEAL
beef burgers with grilled
onions and gorgonzola, 155

arugula, oakleaf, and
basil salad, 95

TO FINISH
cherries with vanilla
mascarpone, 215

TO DRINK
white wine / Pinot Gris

red wine / Malbec

casual dinner
6

TO START
peaches, pluots,
and coppa, 59

THE MEAL
lobster sliders, 66

cucumber, red onion, and dill
shaved salad, 114

TO FINISH
apricot and raspberry
crumble, 220

TO DRINK
aperitif / summer fruit rosé, 25

white wine / Sancerre

red wine / Barbera

casual dinner
8

TO START
grilled figs with
serrano ham, 58

THE MEAL
grilled chicken kebabs, 149

israeli couscous with basil
and mint, 192

watermelon salad with purple
basil and feta, 93

TO FINISH
rose and vanilla
cupcakes, 231

TO DRINK
aperitif / white port and tonic, 17

white wine / Pinot Grigio

red wine / Beaujolais

---

summer menus

---

elegant dinner
4

TO START
grilled apricots with
prosciutto, 59

THE MEAL
spaghettini with lemon-basil
pesto, 143

heirloom tomato fans with
bufala mozzarella, 98

TO FINISH
rosé champagne granita, 222

TO DRINK
aperitif / passion fruit caipirinha, 14

white wine / White Rioja

red wine / Chianti

elegant dinner
8

TO START
chilled watermelon soup
with chile and lime, 86

THE MEAL
grilled scallops with
salmoriglio, 136

panzanella toasts, 179

TO FINISH
poached white peaches with
lemon verbena, 206

TO DRINK
white wine / Prosecco

red wine / Pinot Noir

cocktail party
8

TO DRINK
watermelon and lime
agua fresca, 18

amalfi lemonade, 33

TO PASS
chilled heirloom tomato
soup with cucumber, 87

snapper ceviche, 68

plum and goat cheese tart, 57

cocktail party
12

TO DRINK
papaya and lime
agua fresca, 19

moscato fruit punch, 22

TO PASS
cantaloupe with
bresaola, 58

salt-and-pepper shrimp, 65

bocconcini and toy
box skewers, 98

inspired by **fall**

That first chill in the air means it's harvesttime, and autumn at the greenmarket is unmistakable. There's the sudden appearance of sweet winter squashes, dark, rich greens, sturdy root vegetables, and the last, luscious burst of figs and grapes. Everyone returns from summer trips, and festive indoor gatherings begin again.

FRUITS & NUTS

almonds
apples
Asian pears
chestnuts
crab apples
cranberries
dates
dried fruits
figs
grapes
hazelnuts
olives
pears
persimmons
pistachios
plums
pomegranates
prunes
quinces

VEGETABLES

artichokes
beet greens
beets
black trumpet mushrooms
bok choy
broccoli
broccoli rabe
butternut squashes
cabbage
carrots
chard
chicory
collard greens
Delicata squashes
eggplants
endive
escarole
fennel
frisée
grapes
hedgehog mushrooms
horseradish
Jerusalem artichokes
kale
kohlrabi

leeks
onions
parsnips
porcini mushrooms
potatoes
pumpkins
radicchio
red-leaf lettuce
red sorrel
rutabagas
shallots
shiitake mushrooms
spinach
tomatoes
truffles
turnips
watercress

HERBS

chervil
chives
cilantro
garlic
ginger
marjoram
oregano

parsley
rosemary
sage
thyme

FLOWERS

amaryllis
asters
chrysanthemums
cosmos
dahlias
hydrangeas
lisianthuses
marigolds
ornamental berries
roses and rose hips
salvia
sugar maple leaves
sunflowers
wheat sheafs
zinnias

inspired by **winter**

Because we grew up in England, we are always nostalgic for the winter holidays and our family and friends back home. We've carried our Christmas food traditions here, and we love to sample our friends' traditions, too. When it's cold and blustery outdoors, the only place we want to be is indoors around the table with good friends.

FRUITS & NUTS

apples
Asian pears
bananas
blood oranges
chestnuts
clementines
cranberries
dried fruits
grapefruits
hazelnuts
kumquats
lemons
mandarins
navel oranges
olives
pears
persimmons
pistachios
pomegranates
pomelos
prunes
raisins
tamarillos
tangerines
walnuts

VEGETABLES

beets
bok choy
broccoli
broccoli rabe
Brussels sprouts
butternut squashes
cabbage
cauliflower
celery
celery root
collard greens
Delicata squashes
dried mushrooms
endive
fennel
frisée
horseradish
Jerusalem artichokes
kale
kohlrabi
leeks
onions
parsnips
potatoes
pumpkins
rutabagas
shallots
snow peas
sweet potatoes
turnips
watercress

HERBS

chives
garlic
ginger
parsley
rosemary
sage
thyme

FLOWERS

amaryllis
anemones
camellias
dried flowers
evergreens
forced bulbs
forsythias
fruit blossoms
holly
Iceland poppies
narcissus
ornamental berries
paperwhites
pinecones
ranunculus
star of Bethlehem
tulips

casual dinner
4

TO START
nectarine and prosciutto
crostini, 74

THE MEAL
pepper-crusted tuna
kebabs, 137

sesame-ginger spinach, 173

TO FINISH
poached spiced plums with
vanilla mascarpone, 206

TO DRINK
white wine / Chardonnay

red wine / Cabernet Sauvignon
or Bordeaux

casual dinner
4

TO START
wild mushroom croquetas, 71

THE MEAL
halibut with grapefruit,
parsley, and fennel, 124

parsnip purée, 196

TO FINISH
madagascan white
hot cocoa, 235

TO DRINK
white wine / dry Riesling

red wine / Rosso di Montalcino

casual dinner
6

TO START
mussels with lemon
and ale, 134

THE MEAL
grilled steak with
tomato jam, 156

slow-cooked tuscan
white beans, 182

TO FINISH
mixed berries with
sabayon, 215

TO DRINK
white wine / Gewürztraminer

red wine / peppery Shiraz

casual dinner
8

TO START
grilled halloumi with figs
and blood oranges, 195

THE MEAL
roasted pork loin with
pappardelle, 153

roasted cauliflower with pine
nuts and raisins, 181

TO FINISH
plum, lime, and ginger
crumble, 221

TO DRINK
white wine / Pinot Grigio

red wine / Dolcetto

---

fall menus

---

elegant dinner
4

TO START
delicata squash ravioli, 54

THE MEAL
duck breasts with roasted figs
and balsamic glaze, 162

warm farro salad with
herbs, 192

TO FINISH
late-harvest cheese plate, 203

TO DRINK
white wine / Viognier

red wine / Zinfandel

elegant dinner
8

TO START
charred orange, escarole, and
almond salad, 108

THE MEAL
gnocchi with wild mushroom
topping, 185

squash, mint, and ricotta
salata shaved salad, 115

TO FINISH
praline chocolate truffles, 232

TO DRINK
white wine / Verdiccio

red wine / Pinot Noir

cocktail party
8

TO DRINK
autumn fruit hard cider, 25

cranberry fall warmer, 30

TO PASS
crudités with roasted
eggplant dip, 49

flatbread with radicchio
and fontina, 72

fried artichokes
with aioli, 175

cocktail party
12

TO DRINK
chinatown mule, 26

pom pom, 21

TO PASS
fig, gorgonzola, and arugula
crostini, 75

spanish meatballs with
chorizo and paprika, 77

olives and marcona almonds

casual dinner
4

TO START
endive salad with persimmon
and pomegranate, 89

THE MEAL
seafood linguine with leeks,
fennel, and lemon, 139

crusty bread

TO FINISH
winter cheese plate, 203

TO DRINK
white wine / Sauvignon Blanc

red wine / Sangiovese

casual dinner
4

TO START
pear and gorgonzola tart, 57

THE MEAL
branzino with lemon
and herbs, 127

radicchio, spinach, and
red sorrel salad, 94

TO FINISH
mini bread and butter
puddings, 209

TO DRINK
white wine / Arneis

red wine / Rioja

casual dinner
6

TO START
orange, mint, and hazelnut
salad, 109

THE MEAL
short rib shepherd's pie, 158

roasted broccoli with orange
zest and almonds, 181

TO FINISH
citrus-ginger cake with
orange liqueur glaze, 227

TO DRINK
white wine / Vouvray

red wine / Barolo

casual dinner
8

TO START
trout, watercress, and
apple salad, 104

THE MEAL
ancho pot roast, 161

warm squash salad
with mint, 170

TO FINISH
winter compote with
cinnamon cream, 224

TO DRINK
white wine / Semillon

red wine / Tempranillo

---

winter menus

---

elegant dinner
4

TO START
beet carpaccio, 90

THE MEAL
glazed pork loin with
pear and thyme, 152

chicory and radicchio
gratin, 176

TO FINISH
red wine poached pears, 206

TO DRINK
aperitif / grapefruit fizz, 35

white wine / Pinot Gris

red wine / Merlot

elegant dinner
8

TO START
grapefruit, avocado,
and beet salad, 109

THE MEAL
pork chops with cranberry
beans and thyme, 150

polenta with wild
mushrooms, 196

TO FINISH
chocolate caramel tart, 205

TO DRINK
white wine / Champagne

red wine / Pinot Noir

digestif / spiced hot toddy, 30

cocktail party
8

TO DRINK
ginger and ginger, 14

clementine and campari, 21

TO PASS
crab and cucumber canapés, 63

ham and manchego
croquetas, 71

lemongrass shrimp
skewers, 136

cocktail party
12

TO DRINK
winter red sangria, 25

champagne blush, 35

TO PASS
tuna tartare with sesame, 69

broccoli rabe and parmesan
fritters, 191

lamb kebabs with
pomegranate, 149

some favorite accompaniments

chipotle barbecue sauce

chipotle chiles in adobo sauce 2

canola oil 1 Tbsp

onion ¼ cup minced

garlic 1 large clove, minced

canned crushed tomatoes ½ cup

red wine vinegar ¼ cup

light brown sugar ¼ cup

Worcestershire sauce ¼ cup

orange juice 1 Tbsp

orange zest 1½ tsp grated

fresh thyme ½ tsp chopped

cayenne pepper ½ tsp

salt

makes about ¾ cup

Stem and seed chipotle chiles, then finely chop. In a small saucepan over medium heat, warm canola oil. Add onion, garlic, and chiles and cook, stirring, until fragrant, about 4 minutes. Add tomatoes, vinegar, sugar, Worcestershire sauce, orange juice, orange zest, thyme, and cayenne pepper. Simmer over medium heat, stirring occasionally, until thickened and flavorful, about 20 minutes. Season to taste with salt.

tarragon mustard

Dijon mustard 1 cup

fresh tarragon ½ cup leaves

fresh flat-leaf parsley ½ cup leaves

makes about 1 cup

In a food processor, combine mustard, tarragon, and parsley and process for 2 minutes. Transfer to a bowl and serve. (You can substitute any herbs you like.)

gremolata

garlic 2 cloves

fresh flat-leaf parsley 2 cups leaves

lemon zest 1½ Tbsp grated

extra-virgin olive oil 2 Tbsp

salt and ground pepper

makes about 2 cups

Place garlic cloves on a cutting board, crush lightly, and then chop for 30 seconds. Add parsley and continue to chop for 1 minute. Scrape into a serving bowl, add lemon zest, olive oil, and salt and pepper, and stir to combine. Serve atop or alongside meat, especially veal or lamb, or fish.

tomato jam

tomatoes 5, preferably vine ripened

extra-virgin olive oil 1 Tbsp

red onion ½, thinly sliced

garlic 2 cloves, thinly sliced

ground cumin ½ tsp

ground coriander ½ tsp

fresh ginger ½ tsp grated

cider vinegar ¼ cup

sugar ¼ cup

honey ¼ cup

bay leaf 1

salt and ground pepper

makes about 2 cups

Bring a large pot of water to a boil. Blanch tomatoes for 1 minute then drain, peel, seed, and coarsely chop. Set aside. In a sauté pan over medium heat, warm olive oil. Add onion, garlic, cumin, coriander, and ginger and cook gently, stirring occasionally, until slightly caramelized, about 5 minutes. Add vinegar, sugar, and honey and simmer until reduced and syrupy, about 5 minutes. Add tomatoes and bay leaf and season to taste with salt and pepper. Cover and simmer gently until most of the liquid has evaporated, about 1 hour. Transfer to a bowl and let cool. Serve at room temperature.

red onion and corn salsa

corn 2 ears, shucked

red onion 1, cut into
⅛-inch-thick rings

fresh flat-leaf parsley
1 cup roughly chopped

fresh chives ½ cup finely
snipped

extra-virgin olive oil
¼ cup

Champagne vinegar
1 tsp

salt and ground pepper

makes about 2 cups

Preheat a grill to high and oil grill rack. Grill corn and onion rings until charred on all sides. Cut corn kernels from cobs into a bowl. Roughly chop grilled onion and add to bowl with corn. Add parsley, chives, olive oil, and vinegar and toss to mix. Season to taste with salt and pepper and serve.

salsa verde

extra-virgin olive oil
1 cup

fresh flat-leaf parsley
½ cup leaves

fresh mint ½ cup leaves

bread 1 slice day-old,
torn into pieces

anchovy fillets 2

garlic 2 cloves

capers 1 tsp

lemon zest 1 tsp grated

white wine vinegar
½ tsp

red pepper flakes ½ tsp,
crushed

salt and ground pepper

**makes about
1½ cups**

In a food processor, combine olive oil, parsley, mint, bread, anchovy fillets, garlic, capers, lemon zest, vinegar, and red pepper flakes and process until well blended. Season to taste with salt and pepper and serve.

greek salad on the side

extra-virgin olive oil
½ cup

fresh oregano ¼ cup
small leaves

lemon zest 1½ tsp grated

cherry tomatoes
1½ cups, halved

feta cheese 1 cup
crumbled

salt-cured olives 1 cup

red onion ½, thinly sliced

English cucumber ¼,
thinly sliced

salt and ground pepper

serves 4

In a small bowl, combine olive oil, oregano, and lemon zest and whisk well. In a large salad bowl, combine tomatoes, feta cheese, olives, onion, and cucumber.

Pour dressing over salad, toss to combine, and season to taste with salt and pepper.

croutons

baguette slices 12,
⅛ inch thick

olive oil 1 Tbsp

**makes about
36 croutons**

Preheat oven to 350°F. On a rimmed baking sheet, arrange baguette slices in a single layer and brush lightly on both sides with olive oil. Tear each slice into bite-sized pieces and return to baking sheet. Bake, turning once, until golden brown, 6–8 minutes total. Remove from oven and set aside to cool.

basic techniques

artichokes, trimming: Artichokes start to discolor when cut, so drop them into lemon water after trimming or rub the cut surfaces with a lemon. Using a serrated knife, cut off the top inch of the artichoke to remove the thorns. Using kitchen shears, snip off any remaining thorns. Tear off the smallest, toughest outer leaves. Trim away the bottom of the stem, or trim the stem flush, depending on the recipe. With a vegetable peeler, peel the fibrous outer layer from the stems and where the stems meet the leaves. Depending on the recipe, halve the artichoke and scoop out the fuzzy choke before cooking.

beans, soaking: Dried beans must be soaked before cooking, but they are a better choice than canned beans for recipes in which the beans stand alone. You can soak them for just 4 hours or up to overnight (we sometimes even cheat and soak them for only 2 hours). Pick over the beans and discard any misshapen ones or any small pebbles or grit. Rinse them well, drain them in a colander, and then combine them in a bowl with water to cover by 2 inches. Let soak, then rinse and drain well before cooking.

blanching: This technique is useful for ingredients that need to be softened up just a bit before further cooking, or for cooking an ingredient that will be used as a garnish. It simply means to plunge food into boiling water for a very short time—usually 30 seconds to 1 minute, or as directed in individual recipes. Blanching is also used to loosen the skins of tomatoes and peaches to ease peeling.

blending: Always use caution when you are whirling hot liquids, such as soups, in a blender. You don't want them to spatter all over you and your kitchen. Process the liquid in small batches, taking care not to overfill the blender. Also, always cover the lid with a folded dish towel and hold the lid down firmly before you turn on the blender.

citrus, segmenting: Peeling and segmenting citrus fruits with a knife gives a dish a polished look. Using a chef's knife, cut a slice off the top and bottom of the fruit so it will stand upright. Following the contour of the fruit, slice downward to remove the peel and all of the white pith. Holding the fruit over a bowl, cut along both sides of each segment to free it from the membrane, capturing the segments in the bowl. Or, depending on the recipe, slice the fruit crosswise.

citrus, zesting: Citrus zest is full of flavorful oils that can add a bright flavor to many dishes. Try to buy organic citrus fruits if you plan to use the peel, or scrub the fruit well if it is not organic. To finely grate zest, use a handheld microplane or rasp-style grater that is specifically designed for zesting citrus. Use a zester to make small strips of zest; a vegetable peeler or paring knife works well for removing zest in long strips. In every case, use only the colored part of the peel, avoiding the bitter white pith.

corn, cutting kernels from cob: If needed, trim the stem end so the ear will stand upright. Stand the ear in a shallow bowl and, using a chef's knife, slice down between the kernels and the cob, rotating the ear one-quarter turn after each cut and capturing the kernels and their juices in the bowl.

julienne: This term describes foods, most commonly vegetables, meats, and cheeses, cut into long, thin, narrow strips. To julienne fresh herbs—also known as a chiffonade—stack several leaves, roll up lengthwise into a compact bundle, and thinly slice crosswise.

pomegranate, seeding: To relieve a pomegranate of its juicy seeds, first fill a large bowl with water. Using a serrated knife, cut off a slice from the blossom end, being careful to cut through the pith only, not the seeds. Then score the peel lengthwise into quarters. Pulling from the cut end, break the fruit apart and drop the quarters into the water. Use your fingertips to remove the seeds, which will fall to the bottom of the bowl, then scoop off the peel and pith floating on top and drain.

salting water: When you're cooking pasta or grains, don't hold back when salting the water. For best flavor, it should be very salty, like seawater. Use 1 Tbsp salt for every 2 quarts water.

shrimp, deveining: The intestinal vein in shrimp is edible but unsightly. To remove it, use a paring knife to cut a shallow groove along the back of the shrimp. Lift out the vein with the tip of the knife and discard. Rinse the shrimp under cold running water and drain on paper towels.

squid, cleaning: Whole squid are cheaper than precleaned squid, but they take some work to clean. First pull the head and tentacles away from the body. The innards and ink sac should come away with the head. Reach into the pouch and remove and discard the long, transparent quill. Cut off the tentacles from the head just below the eyes, and discard the head and innards. Squeeze the cut end of the tentacles to remove the hard, round "beak" at the base and discard it. Rinse the squid tentacles and the body inside and out under cold running water, and peel away the gray membrane that covers the pouch.

toasting nuts and seeds: Toasting seeds (and nuts, which are also seeds) brings out their flavor and gives them a lovely appearance. You can do it in the oven at 350°F, but we usually do it on the stove top because it's quicker. You have to keep a close eye on things, and pour the nuts or seeds onto a plate as soon as they turn golden, to stop the cooking. Put the nuts or seeds in a dry frying pan over medium heat and toss and stir occasionally until golden. This will take just a minute for sesame seeds or up to several minutes for hazelnuts or walnuts.

glossary

Asian fish sauce: Called *nuoc mam* in Vietnam and *nam pla* in Thailand, fish sauce is a salty, very pungent seasoning. Used in small amounts, it adds flavor to many Southeast Asian dishes.

basil varieties: When we don't specify a type of basil, we are referring to the familiar green basil (also called Italian or sweet basil). But there are more than 60 other basil varieties. Some of our favorites are Thai basil, lemon basil, the spicy purple (or opal) basil, and dainty bush basil.

bresaola: We love prosciutto and *coppa*, and this is similar, but it's salt-cured, air-dried beef, instead of pork.

chicken stock: We always try to have some homemade chicken stock on hand, but you can substitute purchased. Look for reduced-sodium broth because it gives you more control over the seasoning in a dish.

coppa: This Italian cured meat comes from the shoulder or neck of a pig and is usually served thinly sliced with other cured meats, such as prosciutto (cured ham) and *bresaola* (cured beef).

cucumbers: There is nothing more refreshing than biting into a cool, crunchy cucumber. English (or hothouse) cucumbers are more expensive than the common, waxed slicing cucumber, but they have thinner skins, fewer seeds, and crispier flesh. Long, slender Persian and Japanese cucumbers and smaller, plumper Lebanese cucumbers have even more crunch and better flavor.

endive: Belgian endive, or witloof, is a member of the chicory family with long, torpedo-shaped shoots. The leaves, when pulled apart, are great for dipping for hors d'oeuvres and for tossing in salads. Curly endive, also in the chicory family, is much larger, has narrow, curled leaves, and is used mainly in salads.

escarole: Also known as common chicory, this tangy, leafy green is wonderful grilled or tossed in salads.

mandoline: We use this tool often. It saves time and really adds to the visual presentation of a dish. Mandolines come in a variety of designs and include an assortment of blades that allow you to choose the shape and thickness that suits the food you're cutting.

mirin: A sweet, syrupy Japanese rice wine used only for cooking.

mozzarella cheese: Best known as the cheese you put on pizza, mozzarella is actually quite versatile. Fresh mozzarella, sold floating in whey, has a tangy flavor and stringy texture. *Bocconcini* are small balls of fresh mozzarella, perfect for making *caprese* skewers. *Mozzarella di bufala,* made in Italy from the milk of water buffalo, is rich and creamy and is considered the finest mozzarella available. *Burrata*, which is mozzarella with a cream-filled center, has a buttery flavor and is soft enough to spread.

oakleaf lettuce: The tender, mild-flavored leaves of this salad green look like oak leaves, thus the name. Sometimes the leaves have a red fringe, which adds a handsome color to a salad.

panko: These delicate, crystal-shaped Japanese bread crumbs add a light texture to fried foods. They are sold in well-stocked supermarkets and Asian food markets.

pepitas: Roasted and salted pumpkin seeds, known as *pepitas* (little seeds) in Latin America, are a healthy snack and add flavor and crunch to salads and other dishes.

piquillo peppers: Traditionally grown in Spain, where they are roasted, peeled, and packed in jars or tins, these little peppers add a spicy yet sweet flavor to sauces and are a great topping for flatbreads or bruschetta. Jarred roasted red peppers can be substituted.

poblano chiles: These large and fairly mild chiles are perfect for roasting. Stuff them

with cheese and then roast them to make *chiles rellenos*. If poblanos are not available, Anaheim chiles are a good substitute.

purslane: Some consider purslane a weed, but we think the small, mildly sour leaves are and excellent addition to mixed green salads. Look for this edible succulent in farmers' markets (or in your yard) in summertime.

queso fresco: The name of this Mexican cow's milk cheese translates as "fresh cheese." It is soft and crumbly and similar in taste to ricotta or farmer cheese.

ras el hanout: An aromatic mixure of spices commonly used in North African cooking.

ricotta cheese: A fresh cheese made from either sheep's, goat's, or cow's milk. It's sold in plastic containers and can be used in sweet or savory dishes. *Ricotta salata* is a mild, white sheep's milk cheese that is aged until firm. Feta cheese is a good substitute.

sorrel: A member of the buckwheat family, this sour, juicy salad green has long, spinachlike leaves and woody stems. Look for ruby-streaked red sorrel, a striking addition to a salad.

Sriracha garlic chile sauce: We always have a bottle of this delicious, bright red-orange sauce. Use with caution, as it packs a punch!

Tuscan kale: Also known as *lacinato* or *cavolo nero*, this dark, leafy green can be hard to find outside Italy. Regular kale or dinosaur kale can be substituted.

radicchio: A variety of chicory native to Italy with maroon-splashed leaves and a slightly bitter taste. We love radicchio's versatility: it's great grilled, as a pizza topping, or in a mixed salad. Treviso radicchio is less bitter than other varieties and resembles a large Belgian endive.

sesame seeds: These tiny, flat seeds are used in cooking all over the world (and have been for centuries). We like their nutty flavor and find that they are an ideal garnish for many Asian-flavored dishes. Mix white and black sesame seeds for a striking presentation.

index

Oxmoor
House®

OXMOOR HOUSE

Oxmoor House books are distributed by Sunset Books
80 Willow Road, Menlo Park, CA 94025
Telephone: 650-321-3600 Fax: 650-324-1532

VP and Associate Publisher Jim Childs
Director of Marketing Sydney Webber

Oxmoor House and Sunset Books are divisions
of Southern Progress Corporation

WILLIAMS-SONOMA, INC.

Founder & Vice-Chairman Chuck Williams

COOKING FOR FRIENDS

Conceived and produced by Weldon Owen Inc.
415 Jackson Street, San Francisco, CA 94111
Tel: 415-291-0100 Fax: 415-291-8841
www.weldonowen.com

In Collaboration with Williams-Sonoma, Inc.
3250 Van Ness Avenue, San Francisco, CA 94109

A Weldon Owen Production
Copyright © 2008 Weldon Owen Inc.
and Williams-Sonoma, Inc.

First printed in 2008
10 9 8 7 6 5 4 3 2 1

Library of Congress Cataloging-in-Publication Data
is available.

ISBN-13: 978-0-8487-3288-2
ISBN-10: 0-8487-3288-X

Printed in China by SNP-Leefung

WELDON OWEN INC.

Executive Chairman, Weldon Owen Group John Owen
CEO and President Terry Newell
Senior VP, International Sales Stuart Laurence
VP, Sales and New Business Development Amy Kaneko
Director of Finance Mark Perrigo

VP and Publisher Hannah Rahill
Associate Publisher Amy Marr
Editorial Assistant Julia Nelson

VP and Creative Director Gaye Allen
Associate Creative Director Emma Boys
Designer Lauren Charles
Photo Coordinator Meghan Hildebrand

Production Director Chris Hemesath
Production Manager Michelle Duggan
Color Manager Teri Bell

ACKNOWLEDGMENTS

Alison Attenborough and Jamie Kimm would like to thank their lovely
multi-tasking assistants, Vivian Lui and Lillian Kang; Jessica Boncutter
at Bar Jules; Mary Ellen Weinrib, Lisa Steinmeyer, and Aileen Marr for
loaning gorgeous props; Petrina Tinslay for coming over; Roy Finamore
for good advice; Stephen and *Food & Wine* magazine for encouragement
and opportunity over the years; Jennifer Rubell and Dara Caponigro at
Domino magazine for great encouragement; Aileen Marr, Grace Marr,
Spencer and Boris Lee, Angela Choon, Piers Hanmer, and Joe Maer for
eating; everyone at Weldon Owen who was involved in the project for the
opportunity to make this book; and their parents for encouragement and
letting them escape to the US without giving them a hard time. They would
also like to thank Niman Ranch for their delicious, naturally raised meats;
Chef's Garden for their gorgeous produce; Lobster Place (at Chelsea
Market); and Penn Community Garden.

Photographer Petrina Tinslay
Food Stylists Alison Attenborough and Jamie Kimm
Food Stylist Assistants Vivian Lui and Lillian Kang
Prop Stylists Lauren Hunter and Deborah Williams
Photographer's Assistants Supriya Ruparelia and Erin Richards

Consulting Editors Sarah Putman Clegg and Sharon Silva
Copy Editor Sharron Wood
Proofreaders Lisa Atwood, Linda Bouchard, and Carolyn Miller
Indexer Ken DellaPenta